Chasing Rainbows

Chasing Rainbows

A RECOLLECTION OF THE GREAT PLAINS

1921–1975

BY *Gladys Leffler Gist*

EDITED BY *James Marten*

Iowa State University Press / Ames

JAMES MARTEN IS ASSOCIATE PROFESSOR OF HISTORY
AT MARQUETTE UNIVERSITY, MILWAUKEE, WISCONSIN.

©1993 IOWA STATE UNIVERSITY PRESS, AMES, IOWA 50010
ALL RIGHTS RESERVED

♾ PRINTED ON ACID-FREE PAPER IN THE UNITED STATES OF AMERICA

FIRST EDITION, 1993

Library of Congress Cataloging-in-Publication Data

Gist, Gladys Leffler.
    Chasing rainbows: a recollection of the great plains, 1921–1975/by Gladys Leffler Gist; edited by James Marten. — 1st ed.
        p.   cm.
    Includes bibliographical references.
    ISBN 0-8138-1010-8
    1. Gist family. 2. Leffler family. 3. McCracken family. 4. Torrey family. 5. Gist, Gladys Leffler — Family. 6. Great Plains — Biography. 7. Great Plains — Genealogy. 8. Great Plains — Social life customs. I. Marten, James Alan. II. Title.
CT274.G56G57   1993
929′.2′0973 — dc20   93-10389

TO THE MEMORY OF

GLADYS LEFFLER GIST AND JOSEPH RAYMOND GIST

Contents

Acknowledgments

In an edited work, no less than in a monograph, the author/editor must rely on a number of people for help in sifting through information and tracking down details. I would like to thank for all of their aid the staffs of the inter-library loan office at the Marquette University Memorial Library; the Center for Western Studies at Augustana College, Sioux Falls; the Sioux Falls Public Library; and the Milwaukee Public Library. Individuals who provided favors or information include Barbara Gist, Linda Gist Marten, Kenneth Helder, and Lucille Leivestad. Paula Nelson and John Vogel contributed useful and encouraging comments on the complete manuscript. Bill Silag and the staff at the Iowa State University Press also have been friendly, cooperative, and a pleasure to work with.

I must especially thank the family of Gladys and Raymond Gist, without whose permission and frequent intervention this project could not have been completed. Kent Gist, Rev. Rodney Gist, and Ruth Gist Spencer provided me with copies of their mother's reminiscences, forty years of invaluable account books, unpublished genealogies compiled by Gladys, as well as several years of her personal diaries, and some of their own personal documents. They also answered countless questions, did some reminiscing of their own (unfortunately, too many of their own insights and anecdotes did not end up in the finished product), provided all of the photographs, and demonstrated enthusiasm and confidence that the work would be done well.

It should be noted that I did not approach this project as I have other historical efforts. In fact, I am a historian of the nineteenth-century South and have done most of my research on the experiences of Texans during the sectional conflict and Civil War. Nevertheless, I am a native South Dakotan and retain a great interest in the history of that part of the country. More important, Gladys and Raymond Gist were my wife Linda's grandparents. I never knew Raymond, who died when my wife was only ten, but I did come to know Gladys and had the privilege of being one of her pallbearers when she died in late 1988. Her diary interested me as a historian, and I believe it adds much to our understanding of the period and place in which Gladys lived. In our conversations, Gladys had demonstrated her deep interest in history and I believe she would have approved of my efforts to expose her words and life to a broader audience than just the family.

Although I already have expressed my appreciation to the Gists for their help in nailing down facts and chronologies, I also want to render my thanks for their collective attitude. Through it all, as in the fifteen years I've been married to one of their own, they have treated me not as an in-law but, rather, as a member of the family. They made great efforts to be truthful in their conversations and correspondence about their parents and grandparents, despite blurred memories and some confusion about what it was exactly that I was doing with their mother's "journal" (as it was called within the family). No question was too trivial and they seemed to delight in the information and connections that surfaced during the year or so it took to complete a draft of the edited version. Linda occasionally commented about the novelty of my coming up with tidbits about her family from deep within genealogical essays that Gladys wrote or in newspapers from the towns near where they lived. I thought it was fun, too, and have found it one of the most rewarding efforts I've undertaken during my relatively brief career as a historian. The book is naturally dedicated to the memories of Gladys and Ray, but their descendants must share the gratitude and respect that the dedication carries with it.

Chasing Rainbows

GLADYS
AS A HIGH SCHOOL SENIOR, 1916.

RAY AS A PRIVATE
IN THE 91ST DIVISION, 1918.

INTRODUCTION

It is interesting to know something of our people who have lived before us, and who have been responsible for us being here.

These words written by Gladys Leffler Gist explain her devotion to history and understanding of her place in it. Indeed, Gladys drew her identity from her family, not only from her husband Ray and her children, of course, but also from her historical family, those long lines of Lefflers, McCrackens, Van Hornes, and Sapps from whom she descended. Her compilation of the genealogies and family lore of both the Leffler and the Gist families revealed to her the truth of a verse, from II Timothy 2:20 in the Bible, which she tucked into one of her genealogies: "But in a great house there are not only vessels of gold and silver, but also of wood and of earth; and some to honor, and some to dishonor."

A great variety of "vessels" found their way into the Leffler-Gist genetic warehouse.[1] The Lefflers arrived in New York and Pennsylvania from Bavaria in the early 1800s and eventually ended up in Illinois, where Gladys's grandfather George married Elizabeth Van Horne, the product of seventeenth-century Dutch settlers in New Amsterdam. Their son Frank married Rhodemia McCracken, a native of the Ozarks and a descendant of Scots-Irish pioneers who reached Maryland before the Revolution and eventually made their way into Tennessee, Missouri, and as far west as Texas. The original Gist, Christopher, came to Maryland from England in the 1680s. His family proliferated and spread throughout the South, Appalachia, and the Ohio Valley, and eventually married into yet another set of eighteenth-century settlers, the Torreys, who migrated from England to New England and later into Kentucky.

These descendants of immigrants participated in large and small ways in most of the events that made American history in the eighteenth and nineteenth centuries, just as their own descendants would in the twentieth. They were frontier surveyors and slave overseers, farmers and railroad engineers. They worshipped in frontier sects such as the Methodists and the Baptists (with a few finding their faith in the Presbyterian church). They fought Indians and Englishmen and served in large numbers on both sides of the American Civil War. A Gist served as guide and friend to George Washington in the 1750s, and Torreys followed Daniel Boone into Kentucky and Captain Abraham Lincoln into the Black Hawk War. Ray's father, Burgess, most of whose brothers fought in the Civil War, lay on a frozen hillside as a teenager and listened to the guns at the battle of Pea Ridge in Arkansas in 1862. Gladys's father and grandfather homesteaded for a time in Texas in the early 1890s; on their way back to Missouri, they witnessed the opening of the Cherokee Strip in Oklahoma. Ray fought in France during World War I, and his sons served their country during World War II; the family lived the stereotyped images of prairie hardships during the Great Depression that fell between the wars.

Gladys and Ray were born into these families in 1898 and 1893, respectively. Gladys's father, Frank Leffler, led his family in prayer at the breakfast table each morning and between 1891 and 1907 led them from Missouri to Texas, back to Missouri, then to Oklahoma and on to Iowa. He supported his wife, two sons, and two daughters by farming, butchering, and mending harnesses and shoes. In 1913 the Lefflers moved to a farm near Wheatland, Missouri, but army worms ruined their crops, and in 1915 they returned to Inwood, Iowa, for good, where Frank hauled cream, operated a shoe store, and farmed. He often needed help on the farm during the summers, and occasionally he hired Ray Gist, another Missourian, who had come to northwest Iowa a few years before the Lefflers.

Frank Leffler was a pious, restless, gregarious man. "If friends were counted as riches," the *Inwood Herald* gushed in a 1932 clipping that Gladys preserved, "he would probably be considered the wealthiest man in Inwood." He and his wife Rhodemia provided a secure and supportive environment for their children, which Gladys—a self-professed "Daddy's girl," according to Kent—valued all of her life. Frank, an ardent and lifelong Republican, named his first son (born in 1904) Lee Theodore after the Republican Roosevelt.

Gladys survived three bouts of pneumonia as an infant and young child. She attended school in Wheatland, Missouri, and in Iowa, graduating from Inwood High School in 1916. Gladys was in a class of eight girls, six of whom studied the "normal course" so they could become schoolteachers (college was not a necessary prerequisite for teaching the elementary grades). An old friend, Kenneth Helder, remembered more than seventy years later that she was "a mighty fine gal." Her junior class picture in *The Spectator,* the school yearbook, presents an oval-faced, serious young woman. Unlike the rest of her classmates in the group photograph, who look to the right, Gladys calmly glances to her left. Her "favorite expression" was listed as "Oh, I forgot"; at another point the yearbook has her wanting "someone to keep my glasses on my nose."

A school leader, as treasurer of the "Normal Class" and senior class president, she also sang in the chorus and hosted the seniors' reception for the faculty early in the school year. Gladys joined in most of the young people's social activities, which included picnics on the Big Sioux River, buggy and sleigh rides, parties with games including Post Office and reading the Ouija board, and roller skating. Kenneth Helder and Gladys, who dated for two years, were champion skaters and once won a "masquerade skate" dressed as George and Martha Washington. "We understand," declared her senior yearbook, "that Gladys believes in preparedness and not in waiting as was proven the night of the Leap Year Skate." She and Kenneth fueled the gossip mill as the protagonists in the yearbook's pun-filled "Social Doin's" section, which began, "The other morning Gladys came stalking into the room like a warrior. She said Kenneth Helder the night before and it made her sore." The rest of the story detailed their fictional buggy ride through the countryside, where they met various schoolmates in odd situations.[2]

Whereas Gladys seems to have lived her adolescence in an Iowa village straight out of *The Music Man,* Raymond Gist came to Inwood from a very different background. After the Civil War his father, Burgess, had lived with a brother in Illinois, where he learned barbering and at age thirty married nineteen-year-old Maria Torrey. She bore him nine children over the next twenty-one years, two of whom died in childhood accidents. Early in their marriage Burgess and Maria moved to Wheatland and remained in or near there for the rest of their lives. Burgess barbered until his eyesight faltered, then moved to a forty-acre farm outside of town.

The Gists lived a hardscrabble existence in the hills of southwest Missouri where, it was said, the men were Republicans and the women were Baptists. Money was scarce, and the children began working as soon as they could earn two or four bits for a day's work. As an old woman, the frugal and rather forlorn Maria told Gladys that she hoped to visit a son who had moved to the West Coast. "If I don't get to California before I die," she sighed, "I hope I can get there afterwards." Her children sometimes slipped her money, and Ray once bought her a kitchen range at a time when he could ill afford it. Burgess preferred to stay at home; his daughter-in-law wrote that he was just as happy leaning on a fence watching the hogs as he was doing anything else. He was a demanding and at times harsh father, and most of his children moved away from Missouri when they reached adulthood.

Ray left school after the sixth grade, although he inherited his mother's love of reading. His son Kent called him a "better educated man than he gave himself credit for." Years later, his grandchildren would remember him sitting in his favorite chair, eating lemon drops and reading *National Geographic.* According to Gladys, he attached "Joseph" to his name in honor of a favorite uncle who lived nearby. Although his family called him Ray, he always signed his name "J. R. Gist." By the early 1910s Ray had moved with his younger brother, John, to the greener pastures of northwest Iowa.

Ray and Gladys met when the young Missourian worked for Frank Leffler on his farm west of Inwood. After the Lefflers returned in 1915 from the two-year sojourn in Missouri, the friendship blossomed into courtship. Ray fought in France with the American Expeditionary Force during "The Great War" and was gassed in the Allied offensives of 1918. While overseas, Ray wrote to an uncle that he had seen combat in Flanders and near Verdun and, with characteristic understatement, described the thousands of unburied German soldiers, shell holes, smashed trees, and tangled barbed wire as "certainly . . . a strange sight to see." In another letter he somberly wrote that during a severe bombardment he had been prepared for the "supreme sacrifice [sic]," but he also playfully promised to "tell you about the lassies of France when I return."[3]

Meanwhile, Gladys taught in a country school for a few years, took a bookkeeping course in Sioux City, and waited for letters from Ray. A short stay in Kansas City convinced her that she belonged closer to home, and she returned to Inwood to teach and to keep accounts at the creamery where her father worked. By this time Ray and his brother John had formed a partnership on a rented farm.

Although most of the particulars of their courtship can only be imagined, Ray and Gladys and other young couples in Inwood no doubt enjoyed all the usual small-town activities of the early twentieth century. They went for drives in Ray's Model T Ford, which stalled one night when he was taking Gladys home. The frustrated, embarrassed, and proper young suitor threatened to "push the damn thing onto the railroad tracks and leave it." Another romantic moment turned out more happily. Less than a year after Ray's death, Gladys wistfully recalled in her diary a time in the distant past when "we danced all around that empty school house to the music of that old tin horn phonograph."

Less intimate social opportunities also abounded. In the summer of their marriage, Ray and Gladys could have attended the Farmers' Picnic at nearby Rock Rapids and its free picture shows, baseball game, and "pavement dance"; the local Epworth League's pageant, "The Challenge of the Cross"; a concert by the Calvin College Quartette, which sang a variety of "commendable" songs; and temperance meetings sponsored by the Anti-Saloon League. The highlight of the summer was the Inwood Chautauqua in late June, which promised "snappy mu-

sic" and "great lectures," including the Ojibwa Princess Nea-
wauna. Institute Hall featured movies all year around; "seven
high class pictures" ran in August 1922. The centerpiece of the
winter's entertainment schedule was the annual Farmer's Institute late in January — administered by L. M. Foote, the maternal
grandfather of Gladys and Ray's future daughter-in-law, Doris
Leivestad — which featured livestock, poultry, crop, and baked
goods competitions, as well as lectures, debates, and presenta-
tions on agricultural issues and methods. At the 1924 Institute
Ray won the five-dollar prize for first place in the contest for the
best ten ears of white corn and a two-and-a-half dollar prize for
the third-best single ear.[4]

On the second Sunday in June 1921, they were married,
beginning a life together that would, in the long tradition of
both of their families, represent those average Americans who
dealt with the storms and calms of American history. More than
four decades later, two years before Ray's death and toward the
end of her reminiscences, Gladys reflected on contemporary society, a society so different from that in which she began her life.
She wrote, not altogether approvingly, of two-income and two-
car families and "a generation on the run." Everyone seemed to
be "working for more education, more entertainment, more of
everything." "Chasing rainbows," she called it. "People have
been like that ever since Adam and Eve," she admitted. "We just
have more ways to run now and more rainbows to chase."
Gladys pursued a few rainbows herself during her long life, and
she described the chases in her reminiscences.

The stories Gladys tells offer insights into a number of rural, twentieth-century phenomena.[5] These accounts demonstrate
how the rapidly changing technology of the twentieth century
affected individual Americans, as we see the Gists travel in
horse-drawn buggies as well as jet planes, as they store food in
underground "caves" and electric refrigerators, and as they hun-
ker down beside a radio in the 1920s and in front of a television
set in the 1950s. Gladys relished these changes, for the most
part, and her reminiscences easily convince the reader that the
family's standard of living improved dramatically despite two
decades of economic uncertainty and crisis.[6]

The Gists' experiences mirrored those of millions of other
rural Americans during the Depression and war years; their for-

tunes rose and fell with their country's, representing a microcosm of these great social and economic shifts. Ray and Gladys experienced firsthand what Gilbert Fite calls the "vast and fundamental changes" that began to emerge in American agriculture in the 1920s. "The application," posits Fite, "of new technology, chemistry, and plant and animal sciences began to accelerate, producing changes more important than anything that had ever happened in the history of American farming." By the 1940s and 1950s "the evolutionary changes of former years . . . became of such fundamental importance as to be called revolutionary."[7] The effects of this revolution can be measured in the lives of the Gists.

Yet another valuable aspect of Gladys's work is that it records the lives of tenant farmers and provides evidence that tenant farming, in at least some instances, was neither the stepladder to land ownership nor the economic deadend that scholars have frequently labeled it. Thousands of South Dakotans shared the Gists' tenuous relationship with individual parcels of land, as farm tenancy in the state soared from 21.8 percent in 1900 to nearly half of all farmers in 1935.[8]

Too often, late February found the Gists packing up and moving on. Carl Hamilton, who grew up in an Iowa tenant family, recalled the worries and tensions and inconveniences caused by their own frequent moves. Dishes were always broken; rugs never quite fit in the new house; they always had too much or too little furniture. Years after they finally settled on their own farm, his mother would comment every March about the "poor people who are having to move."[9] Yet the Gists, who experienced the same seminomadic existence, rarely felt like marginal participants in the farm economy or in the communities in which they lived.

Perhaps most important, Gladys's narrative presents in rich detail the everyday life of a farm family. Although there never was a Gist family farm whose passing must be mourned in the late twentieth century, the Gists personify those "rural values"— determination, communal spirit, modesty, hard work—that are often touted but rarely explained in the modern-day United States. Just as Gladys's reminiscences provide many examples of the dizzying changes that have occurred since the 1920s—for instance, farm families declined from a quarter of the popula-

tion in 1935 to just over 6 percent in 1965—they also supply
ample evidence of the continuity of attitudes, values, and experiences in the American heartland.[10] The seasonal patterns of
planting and harvest shape the rhythms of this document; the
growth and maturation of the Gist children offer poignancy; the
vivid demonstrations of rural community life and culture provide texture; and Ray's battles with ill health lend it a bittersweet
quality.

On the other hand, Gladys's comments about politics, although sometimes enlightening, are so rare that a reader would
not guess that she and Ray were both adamant Republicans. She
never wrote about farmers' groups such as the radical Farm
Holiday Association or the more moderate Farmers' Union. A
teetotaler, she apparently never felt the need to write about Pro-
hibition. Except for World War II and a few lines on the Peace
Movement in the 1960s, American foreign policy remains
largely absent; she failed to mention even once the Korean War,
for example, or the Soviet Union. Perhaps one should not expect a South Dakota farm wife to place much importance on her
feelings about politics or foreign policy. Although Gladys, who
usually formed an opinion on most subjects, did concern herself
with current events and crises, years later she preferred to write
about things that had given her pleasure, such as family activities and friendships, or about outside forces that had directly
affected her life, such as the dust storms or the world war that
drew her sons into the U.S. Army.

Gladys wrote her reminiscences as a yearly summary of
important events. She apparently kept a diary during at least
some of her life, and to write her personal history she drew on
those diaries, on her farm account books, and on her impressive
memory. Internal evidence suggests that she began writing her
reminiscences around 1960 and continued adding to them over
the years. By the late 1960s, it seems, she was writing shortly
after the events she described. Well before her death in 1988, she
distributed copies of the reminiscences to her three children,
who had been unaware of the extent of her writing.

Although she chose to express herself in this form rather
than in a detailed diary, her writing shares certain characteristics
with the diaries of other western women. Lillian Schlissel suggests that these documents were in effect family histories, "sou-

venir[s] meant to be shared like a Bible, handed down through generations, to be viewed not as an individual's story but as the history of a family's growth and course through time."[11] Yet, the years between the events and Gladys's depiction of them served, as Joanna Stratton observed about the memoirs she edited, "to deepen the insight and heighten the perspective of the writers."[12]

Gladys presents a generally optimistic view of her and her family's lives, despite occasional crushing disappointments and extreme hardships, because she believed that things do indeed turn out all right. Nevertheless, her dependence on other sources to complement what may have been, at times, rose-colored memories, provided details and renewed emotions, making her less inclined to obscure fears, concerns, or sadness. Simply put, her reminiscences accomplish what Elizabeth Hampsten found to be a great strength in personal letters of North Dakota women: They "confirmed what everybody knows, that life is complicated and difficult, funny and sad at the same time."[13] As these and other historians of western women have argued for years, studying the lives and attitudes of common Americans — particularly women — has value. In this way Gladys Leffler Gist's reminiscences can help light the hazy and often convoluted path from her past to our present.[14]

EDITOR'S NOTE

Gladys's original reminiscence consisted of slightly more than 150 pages of surprisingly legible, tightly formed longhand that bears very few crossouts or revisions. Gladys was a fairly educated person, but some spelling and grammatical errors did sneak into her manuscript. I have alerted the reader to them or changed them only when clarity demanded it. I have added apostrophes to possessives, which Gladys rarely provided, and have spelled out some abbreviations (for state names and words such as "doctor"). Except for these minor alterations, the text appears exactly as it did in the original. From time to time, my own comments — about something Gladys mentions in her diary or about the background of events in her life — are included within Gladys's text. These comments of mine are set off by brackets and appear in italic type. In addition, I have provided a general introduction to each chapter.

A quaint idiosyncrasy of Gladys's generation of rural mid-westerners — and one shared at times by the editor, who grew up in small towns in southeastern South Dakota — is to pluralize the first name of the head of household when talking about an entire family. For instance, Gladys often tells about trips to "Kents" or about "Monts" coming to visit. She means, of course, that she and Ray visited Kent, Edith, and their children, or that Ray's brother Mont and his wife Rena came calling; her use of the "s" does not indicate a possessive in this case, and I have tried to differentiate true possessives from simple plurals. Normally I have not identified members of the Gist or Leffler families, unless Gladys leaves pertinent information unstated. The family tree identifies several generations of both sides of the family. The notes at the end of each chapter provide the usual supporting information relevant to events or people or issues that show up in Gladys's reminiscences. When possible, I have also taken advantage of the Gists' surviving farm records to flesh out her references to their financial situation. Uncited information was drawn from one of four sources: Gladys's farm account books, conversations or correspondence with living family members, Gladys's genealogical compilations, or her diaries from the years 1964–1978.

NOTES

1. These family histories come primarily from Gladys's own unpublished compilations, and from Jean Muir Dorsey and Maxwell Jay Dorsey, comps., *Christopher Gist of Maryland and Some of His Descendants, 1679–1957* (Chicago: John S. Swift, 1969), 1–5, 16–17. Gladys told some of the same stories to two different interviewers in a Dakota State College oral history series. The family possesses copies of both, dated 1977 and 1983.

2. Kenneth Helder interview, Inwood, Iowa, July 7, 1989; *The Spectator* (Inwood: Inwood Herald Print, 1915 and 1916).

3. Ray to Mr. and Mrs. Robert Torrey, December 25, 1918, and January 6, 1919, courtesy of Rev. Rodney Gist.

4. *Inwood Herald,* June 16 and July 21, 1921; August 24 and January 19, 1922; February 14, 1924.

5. Gladys's reminiscences fit into the flurry of recent books—published primary sources as well as secondary works—describing the distinctive lives of western women. They range from Lillian Schlissel's *Women's Diaries of the Westward Journey* (New York: Schocken Books, 1982) and Sandra L. Myres's *Westering Women and the Frontier Experience, 1800–1915* (Albuquerque: Univ. of New Mexico Press, 1982) to compilations such as Joanna L. Stratton's *Pioneer Women: Voices From the Kansas Frontier* (New York: Simon and Schuster, 1981) and Christine Fischer's *Let Them Speak for Themselves: Women in the American West, 1849–1900* (Hamden, Conn.: Shoe String Press, 1977). Janet Lecompte discovered the voice of an urban, working class western woman in *Emily: The Diary of a Hard-Worked Woman* (Lincoln: Univ. of Nebraska Press, 1987), and Marlene and Haskell Springer published a diary that brings one woman's story into the twentieth century in *Plains Woman: The Dairy of Martha Farnsworth, 1882–1922* (Bloomington: Indiana Univ. Press, 1986).

For a useful discussion of the literature on western women, see Elizabeth Hampsten, *Read This Only to Yourself: The Private Writings of Midwestern Women, 1880–1910* (Bloomington: Indiana Univ. Press, 1982). For critiques of the historiography on western women, see Susan Armitage, "Through Women's Eyes: A New View of the West," in Susan Armitage and Elizabeth Jameson, eds., *The Women's West* (Norman: Univ. of Oklahoma Press, 1987), 9–18, and Sandra L. Myres, "Women in the West," in Michael P. Malone, ed., *Historians and the American West* (Lincoln: Univ. of Nebraska Press, 1983), 369–86. One of the most useful analyses of the lives of western women in the nineteenth century — whose experiences Gladys's often resembled — is Glenda Riley, *The Female Frontier: A Comparative View of Women on the Prairie and the Plains* (Lawrence: Univ. Press of Kansas, 1988).

More applicable to the later part of Gladys's life is Deborah Fink's *Open Country, Iowa: Rural Women, Tradition and Change* (Albany: State Univ. of New York Press, 1986), which studies women's roles in and responses to community, kinship, technological change, and agricultural production in the twentieth century, with an emphasis on the post–World War II period. Fink justifies her book with the obvious but nevertheless often overlooked concept that "women have been major participants and have stories to tell that will clarify the events that have shaped rural life and made it distinctive" (p. 7).

6. Gladys probably would not have agreed with Ruth Schwartz Cowan, who has argued that despite mechanization, most American women work harder now to maintain their households than their great-grandmothers did because of the almost complete elimination of servants in middle-class homes, changing standards of cleanliness, and the increasing pace of everyday life — as reported in her book *More Work for Mother: The Ironies of Household Technology from the Open Hearth to the Microwave* (New York: Basic Books, 1983). Katherine Jellison points out that, although the new technologies actually may have increased the time farm women spent doing housework, they also have improved the quality of their lives dramatically; this accounting is given in "Women and Technology on the Great Plains, 1900–1940," *Great Plains Quarterly* 8 (Summer 1988): 145–57.

7. Gilbert C. Fite, *American Farmers: The New Minority* (Bloomington: Indiana Univ. Press, 1981), 69. Fite applies these and other themes directly to South Dakota in "The Transformation of South Dakota Agriculture: The Effects of Mechanization, 1939–1964," *South Dakota History* 19 (Fall 1989): 278–305. For an analysis of the forces acting on agriculture in Iowa and in California, especially since the Second World War, see Mark Friedberger, *Farm Families and Change in Twentieth-Century America* (Lexington: Univ. Press of Kentucky, 1988).

8. W. F. Kumlien, "A Graphic Summary of the Relief Situation in South Dakota (1930–1935)," Bulletin 310, (Brookings: Agricultural Experiment Station, South Dakota State College, 1937), 46.

9. Carl Hamilton, *In No Time at All* (Ames: Iowa State Univ. Press, 1974), 4–8, quote on 6. For a short summary of the debate over the ramifications of farm tenancy, see Donald L. Winters, *Farmers Without Farms: Agricultural Tenancy in Nineteenth Century Iowa* (Westport, Conn.: Greenwood Press, 1978), 3–9.

10. Fite, *American Farmers,* 101.

11. Schlissel, *Women's Diaries,* 11.

12. Stratton, *Pioneer Women,* 25–26.

13. Hampsten, *Read This Only to Yourself,* 102.

14. Collections of family farm records similar to the Gists' provide the sorts of information called for by Everett Edwards many years ago in "The Need for Historical Materials for Agricultural Research," *Agricultural History* 9 (January 1935): 2–11.

GLADYS AND RAY IN THE EARLY 1920s.

CATCHING ROOT, 1921–1925

Ray and Gladys began nearly half a century of marriage on a 320-acre farm west of Inwood, Iowa, not far from the meandering Big Sioux River. During the next five years, they would live on two other nearby farms before their big move to western South Dakota. These first years, as in the initial stages of any marriage, saw them establish a relationship—duties, routines, modes of interaction—that would grow over the next forty-six years. They also revealed the character and personality traits that would shape their responses to the crises they faced and fix their reputations in three different communities.

Throughout their lives, relatives, friends, and acquaintances described Ray and Gladys as honest, responsible, cautious, and unassuming. In its June 16, 1921, report of their wedding, the *Inwood Herald* praised the "popular newlyweds." Gladys, said the paper, had worked locally as a teacher and as a clerk at the Inwood Creamery, and had contributed to the Methodist Church by teaching Sunday School and as a member of the Epworth League. "Without any special commotion," declared the *Herald,* Gladys "has been a quiet and positive force in all these things." Since Ray's arrival "some years ago," the article continued, he "has won for himself the respect and confidence of . . . the community," which has "always considered [him] a good man and reliable." Five years later, when the Gists left for western South Dakota, the *Herald* (February 4, 1926) "regret-[ted] to see such fine young people . . . leave our community."

When they went out, Ray and Gladys socialized with neighbors or with family. Ruth Gist Spencer wrote just after her

mother's death that Gladys "would have liked to be more social,
but Dad was pretty hard to move." She did not recall them going
to a movie, a dance, or a sporting event. "Their social life was
entirely with their neighbors and visiting back and forth with
friends and relatives." Threshing season brought friends and
family together every summer; Ray would even sip a beer on
those exhausting but happy occasions. In Iowa, Gladys and Ray
joined the Lyon Township Agricultural Club, comprised of fifteen or so young couples who met on a monthly basis to discuss
farm methods and to have fun. Meetings rotated among members' homes. When a colleague married, the club held a shivaree
and gave the couple a rocking chair.[1] Son Kent reported that the
family often spent evenings playing Rook, Chinese Checkers, or
Monopoly. Scarcely a year went by that the Gists did not undertake a major automobile trip to see family in Iowa, Illinois,
Missouri or, much later, Idaho and Washington.

A basic decency—an "urgent honesty," in their son Rodney's words—shaped both of their personalities. Late in her life
Gladys only half-jokingly exclaimed to Ruth that she was "glad
that no one in her family had ever been in jail." Kent and Rodney both witnessed memorable examples of their father's integ-
rity. Once, as a youngster, Kent found some old rusty horseshoes
at a neighbor's place and brought them home. "I considered
them of no value to the neighbor," he wrote fifty years later, but
"Dad had a different opinion, and I found myself taking them
back with an apology." On another occasion, during World War
II, Rod was loading and weighing the grain harvest. When he
loaded the landlord's one-third share, he tightened the chain on
the side of the wagon and "fluffed up" the load, making it
lighter than it might otherwise be, although it appeared to be
full. Ray observed this and lectured Rod—with words that
found their way into more than one sermon after Rod became a
Methodist minister—on his definition of honesty. "I know that
the neighbors got more than we've got," he declared, "but I
never knowingly cheated anybody for anything I've got. . . .
The landlord owns this place and is entitled to one-third of the
crop and I want it divided correctly right down to the last
bushel. . . . If you can't do it, let me know and I'll find some-
body who can."

Kent has said that "my parents were people who believed

that every person needed to be responsible for his own life and actions." The boys remembered only one piece of fiscal advice from their parents, which Ray and Gladys lived by throughout their lives: "If you don't have it, don't spend it." The children learned their economic lessons through farm projects their parents gave them — potato patches, lambs, calves — that enabled them to earn their own money.

Other characteristics of the parents come through in the memories of the children. Rod remarked that whereas Ray was perceived as a gentle, quiet man, Gladys presented a harder front. She once told him, "Your Dad has more compassion in his little finger than I have in my whole body." Even so, Gladys dutifully cared for ill and downtrodden relatives and in-laws and after Ray's death volunteered for a number of community services including, in her seventies, working as a "gray lady" at a nursing home.

Gladys also occasionally revealed a subtle sense of humor. At one point she writes about toddler Rodney's close encounter with a large snake. "Even a little garter snake terrifies me," she declared, but "so far I have been able to out run them." Many years later, when old age had made her memory unreliable, she ended a pleasant conversation with her granddaughter's mother-in-law — to whom she had spoken several times over the years — by saying, "I don't know who you are, but we sure had a good visit."

Despite these glimpses of her sympathetic nature, Kent remembered his mother as a "worry wart" who, he feared, "missed some of the good times by worrying too much about all the things that could go wrong." Whereas Gladys earned respect from the people who knew her, Ray was more likely to inspire affection. He was not a community leader and rarely accepted leadership positions. Although he served as Sunday School superintendent in Presho, South Dakota, he usually let others organize community or church functions. Both parents hated their inability (at least before the 1940s) to provide their children with more than the bare necessities. Gladys cried when Kent, as senior class president, had to crown the homecoming queen wearing a sweater rather than a proper suit. Ray could not always spare fifty cents whenever his teenaged eldest son asked for it, but insisted on selling a load of grain in the late 1930s so Kent could buy a nine-dollar class ring.

Despite the stern economy forced on the Gists during these long, hard times, Gladys at least always had time for music, which provided a constant theme in her life. From her days in the Inwood Methodist Church and high school choirs continuing through her violin lessons as a septuagenarian, Gladys loved any kind of music. Her most prized possessions always included a piano or a violin, and she insisted that her children pursue musical knowledge at one level or another. Kent played a variety of instruments, Ruth and Rodney learned the violin, and all three took piano lessons, although only Ruth became much of a pianist. The family sang together—"from the time we could talk," according to Kent—and sometimes played in pick-up "orchestras" with neighbors. Gladys always included a category for "Music and Entertainment" in her yearly summaries of the farm accounts, even when the outlay for both totaled only a dollar or two for an entire year. Music was Gladys's only purely creative outlet, aside from the writing she did late in her life, and certainly one of the few "luxuries" she enjoyed.

In all things, their children unanimously recalled, Ray and Gladys were partners. Although Ruth "never heard them raise voices in anger or, at the other end of the spectrum, show any physical affection for each other," she knew that "a very deep respect and devotion" had grown between them. Kent "never hear[d] them speak a cross word to each other" and suspected that when they did disagree, "they carefully shielded (us) from those occasions." Even in the toughest times, "my parents were always able to make us feel secure, even though . . . they had their own misgivings." Perhaps the most accurate description of their relationship, as the diary portrays it, is Rod's: They were "well-mated."

The parents rarely displayed emotion or love publicly, and they never spoke to their children of matters relating to sex. Nine-year-old Kent, for instance, did not know of the imminent arrival of his second sibling until the day Ruth was born in March 1931. Ray would take the children down to the barn to witness the birth of livestock, but that was about as far as sex education went in the family. A scandal concerning Uncle Marion Gist, Ray's handsome older brother, who "got a girl in trouble" and escaped Fairview, South Dakota, a step ahead of the sheriff, went unmentioned by Gladys for decades.

In these and other matters Ray and Gladys presented, in Ruth's words, "a solid front" to their children, and their conduct of their farming business also reflected a basic solidarity and mutual trust. Rod suggested that Gladys kept abreast of the needs of and developments on the farm, and believed that his father, appreciating Gladys's good business judgment, cleared most decisions with her. His confidence in her—Kent believed that Ray "was always a little in awe of being married to a former schoolteacher"—and her experience led him to rely on Gladys to manage the books. Gladys sat down on the first of every month to catch up on the accounts, which she faithfully kept for more than forty years.

The first five years in Iowa began an odyssey for the Gists that would take them through three major relocations and a number of lesser moves. They would make the first of those moves in Iowa, have their first child, and begin to build a base for their future. They would also enjoy a prosperity they would not know again until after the Second World War. They spent Gladys's savings from teaching country school for five years on new furniture, a sewing machine, a set of china, an oriental rug, and the possession that Gladys seemed to treasure most, a white and chrome enamel cookstove. These were happy and relatively trouble-free years, a pleasant interlude before the harsh realities of depression and war.

1 9 2 1

We were married June 8, 1921, in the home of my parents in Inwood, Iowa, at 4 o'clock in the afternoon. We were 28 and 23 years of age and old enough and mature enough to try and work for understanding.

Forty years, three children, and considerable "for better and for worse" later, I now know what being "madly in love" is. It either burns itself out into a handful of ashes, or it catches root and is cherished into a steady glow of abiding love. St. Paul tells us how to nurture the mad love of the beginning, in the thirteenth chapter of Corinthians.

We were married by our Methodist Minister, Rev. Thaddeus S. Basset, and Fred and Anna Hanson signed the marriage license as witnesses. We chose the simplest ceremony in the hymnal rituals, standing without attendants in a little alcove in one corner of the living room. This was made of white sheets, trimmed with pink ribbon and garden flowers. The peonies and roses were in bloom and the whole house was decorated with loving care.

We had about thirty guests, relatives and close friends. Lue Dema Wattenbarger played Mendelssohn's wedding march on the piano as we came down the stairs together and walked to the alcove. Ray wore a dark blue suit and my bridal gown which I had made myself was of white canton crepe de chine trimmed with pearl beads. It was made with a scalloped overskirt and plain waist. I wore a three quarter length veil and my bridal bouquet was of pale pink roses from the greenhouse.

Our neighbors and four of my closest girl friends served us a three course wedding dinner at two long tables in the dining room and adjoining end of living room. I do not remember the menu, but I do remember that I accidentally spilled my glass of water on the table linen. I shall always be grateful to my friend Ella who was serving us. She quickly brought a large linen napkin and covered the spot so it didn't even show. It covered a little of my embarrasment too.

After dinner we were gathered in groups out on the lawn, visiting and making merry, when by pre-arrangement Olaf Leivestad and Esther Erickson drove up in his car and sticking a gay package out the window called, "You will have to come and get it." We walked over to the car, jumped in the back seat and away we went. They took us to Hudson, S.D., two stations south, and left us there. The next day we returned to Fairview by train where John met us and took us home. That was our honeymoon.[2]

Our first home was a rented ½ section farm owned by

Jas. Mulhall of S[ioux] City.[3] It was on the Iowa side of the
[Big Sioux] River in the edge of the hills east of Fairview, S.
D. Ray and John had moved in the first of March and
batched [*were bachelors*] up to that time. It was a cozy little
house and we had spent many happy hours planning and buying furniture. Ray had painted the woodwork and scrubbed it
clean and I had saved enough teaching money to buy nice
furniture, so it was a dream home to begin with. He had his
car all paid for, a Model T Ford with a specially made maroon colored body. Real classy.

We bought the most beautiful cook stove (range) that I
had ever seen, as advertised in "The Country Gentleman." It
was a white enamel and chrome Sanico, with a blue steel
cooking top. There was a warming oven above the top and a
big reservoir on the end for hot water. We had a piano, red
gum wood bedroom suite, wool rug, oriental pattern, New
Home sewing machine, new linoleums, an assortment of
chairs, two extra beds and bedding. Nearly all new kitchen
utensils from showers and gifts and we bought a 100 piece set
of china from Sears Roebuck, white with a blue decorative
line around the edge. The bank loaned us the money for machinery, 8 horses and 10 milk cows so we were off to a good
start.

We needed so many things that first summer that we soon
found that our cream checks wouldn't buy everything. We
determined not to run any store bills so began rigid economy.
Fortunately we had enough clothes to last a long time. We had
an old buggy so often drove . . . that on the road to save
buying gasoline. It was two years before we could drive the
car freely. One year, 1922, we did not even get a license for it.

Our crops were only fair that first year and prices
dropped very low. Oats were $.18 and corn $.27. We paid a
share rent of grain but were to pay $8 an acre for hilly pas-
ture and were unable to raise all the payment for that when it
came due.

We had the opportunity to rent Ben Brown's farm for the

next year so we decided to move, giving a note for the unpaid rent. This was 240 A. of better land and buildings and not so much pasture.

By Christmas we knew that I was pregnant and I spent the next 6 weeks with horrible nausea, and as I couldn't even keep medicine down soon became too weak to do my housework. After 6 wks I began to improve and felt OK.

1 9 2 2

About March first we moved to our new home, 2 miles west, two south and ¼ east of Inwood. It was a large 8 room house. We had a dining room so bought a round oak dining table and sectional book case at a sale and new linoleum to furnish it. The house was hard to heat so in winter we only heated two rooms. The men sawed wood and we used corn cobs for fuel. It wasn't so bad that spring as the weather soon warmed, but the next winter after the baby came it was pretty rough. We just had a little heating stove about the size of a five gallon cream can and I was forever poking cobs in it. I never hated anything like I did that stove.

Our first baby, Kent, was the big event of that year. The men were stacking the oats and working at the neighbors the week before he was born. We had a telephone but they didn't so Ray came home every noon to see how I was. The time was overdue! Kent was born about 4 A.M. Aug 12, 1922. Mrs. Henry Anderson came with . . . Dr. Stewart to help us. There were no maternity hospitals anywhere near then. The baby weighed 9 lb so I guess I ate enough after all. Doctor didn't mention diet. Mrs. Anderson returned home with the doctor, and Anna Helder a widow with two small children helped us for about two weeks. We paid her $1 a day and the dr. bill for delivery was $15. [Gladys's older sister] Ethel gave me [her son] Lloyd's outgrown baby clothes so Kent wasn't wrapped in swaddling clothes but he didn't have any new ones except diapers either. I dreamed of one nice new blanket but funds only stretched enough to pay Anna. Later on I made him a soft white bunting bound with blue satin so usually when we are denied something we want real bad it is only temporary and something even better comes along.

We kept the baby in the big kitchen most of the time that winter and I guess we kept him warm as he grew and was healthy and happy.

Crops were good that year and we were able to begin to pay off some of our bank loans. The first check went to Mr. Mulhall for the back rent we owed him. By return mail came a check for $5.00 to buy the baby something so we started a savings fund for him. Ray did some home barbering for a few of the neighbor boys, never making any charge, and they often dropped a coin in Kent's bank so his fund grew in that way.

1 9 2 3

We reinstated our Ford car by getting a license for the roads and for the next three years we used it a lot. I didn't drive it much because it had to be cranked by hand to start and it was pretty temperamental.

A shopping trip to Sioux Falls, thirty miles away was an event that did not happen to us very often.[4] That fall I needed a new coat so we decided to spend a day there shopping. We got all fixed up ready to go and the Ford wouldn't start. Ray and John both wore themselves out coaxing and cranking, finally hitched a horse on it and pulled it but to no avail. We gave up and stayed home. That was one of several times when Ray vowed he would never own another Ford. He kept his

word until [in] 1959 a blue & ivory Fairlane Ford caught his
eye and before we had driven it two years we were in a collision that put us both in a hospital and smashed the Ford beyond repair. We replaced it with another Ford, by that time
we were too old for superstition. They just can't all be
jinx[ed].

In August we went to visit my girlhood chum, Eula
Boone near Red Oak, Iowa, for a week end. Kent was a year
old and we had his hair cut straight across the front like
bangs. She nearly had a fit! Her baby was a girl but she said
if she had a boy he would have a man's hair cut. Kent soon
got one. Eula never had a boy but now has six grandsons and
no granddaughters. Sometimes you have to wait a long time
for what you want.

We attended church and belonged to the LTAC (Lyon
Township Agricultural Club) of young married couples where
we had great times.[5] We furnished our own entertainment at
each meeting with a program of music, discussions, debates,
etc., and just plain hilarious fun. We always took the baby
along and so did everyone else. There were more children than
grown ups in our club. I also belonged to an extension club
and worked diligently at whatever we were supposed to do.[6]
We each made a dress form of a thin T shirt and heavy brown
paper tape. The girls stuck it on you like a cast, then cut it off
up the center with a razor blade and stuck it together again.
We mounted it on yardsticks and a base and were all ready to
design a wardrobe. Nettie Helder fainted when we got her
encased so we had to lay her out like a corpse and bring her
to before we could get the form off.

We got a new heating stove that fall that would burn any
kind of fuel and it was large enough to give steady heat. We
used wood for economical reasons.

We paid $2000 cash rent for the farm and realized a fair
profit.

1 9 2 4

This was a good year. We had good crops and no serious financial reverses. After harvest we made a trip to Wheatland, Missouri, to visit Ray's parents and the Leffler and McCracken relatives. Ethel and Raymond and family went with us, we in our red Ford and they in a Willys Overland. We got lost from each other before we got to Sioux City and had quite a time staying together. [T]he roads were nearly all gravel or dirt. We got to Missouri Valley, Iowa, the first day and camped overnight in our tent. From there on to Council Bluffs the road was about 4 inches thick with dust and sometimes visibility was nil. We swallowed and coughed and the men smoked to clear their lungs but Ethel & the kids and I relied on nature's good old remedy — spit.

We got to Kansas City the second day and camped in a park. There was a utility house there for campers where we could put a nickel in a meter and get enough gas to cook breakfast if we hurried. We got to Wheatland the next day.[7] I had never met [Ray']s parents and wanted to look nice. I must have, after those three days with a baby, but it was fun. [La]-Mont and Rena, Ray's brother and wife from Illinois, were there when we arrived. I told Mother Gist it must be wonderful to have six grown sons and two daughters. She said, "I hope I can live long enough to get them all under our roof at one time again." She never had that privilege. They were all at her funeral in 1927.

While we were there Father Gist expressed a wish to see his old birthplace and home near Fayetteville, Ark., so Mont, Rena, Charles and us took two cars and took them to Fayetteville. If we had only asked him about his ancestry and early life then! He located his old home which was hardly recognizable after 60 years and found the cemetery where his father Andrew was buried but it was unkept. He located the grave but the rock marker was not legible. We stayed overnight in tourist cabins then back to Wheatland the next day. Our two

weeks were all too short with so many relatives on both sides
to visit. We talked and feasted and enjoyed every minute of it.

Grandma Minerva Ann McCracken came home with
Ethel and Raymond and Fred Gist came with us to look for a
new location.[8] His wife Della fought another move in every
way that she could but Fred was a "greener pastures" man.
Della told me later that they had moved 18 times in 20 years.

We were really tired when we got home. John had
batched while we were gone and I expected to find evidence of
it but my good neighbor had been there the day before and
had the house all shining clean. It looked like heaven.

In October John and Fred went back to Missouri in the
red Ford and brought Della and their six children back with
them. We helped him find a job working for Tom Riley on a
farm near Rock Valley [Iowa]. He stayed there about a year
then moved back to Missouri on the train. The men bought
our first tractor, it was a used Waterloo, a big clumsy thing,
and John broke his arm trying to crank it before they got it
home. It was not very satisfactory so they continued to farm
with horses.[9]

In December John married Mathilde Dahlstrom, a Nor-
wegian girl who had come from Norway in 1920 and was living with her aunts near Inwood. She was a pretty girl of 18
years.

1 9 2 5

Ray and John continued their partnership farming so we all
lived together for this year. Mathilde and I tried hard to be
considerate of each other and we got along fine. It was harder
for her as I was established there and our ways were many of
them different than she had known in Norway. She had been
in America four years tho and had worked some as a maid.
She was a good cook and anxious to learn American ways.

Freds were having such a hard time with their big family, so
we kept one of their boys, Junior, who was 9 years old, and
sent him to the country school near us.[10] That made us a family of six. Kent was past two and got plenty of attention. We
nearly always took him with us wherever we went to give
John and Mathilde a chance to enjoy being alone.

We raised a big garden, kept a few chickens and the men
milked 10–12 cows. They had 27 sows and raised 145 pigs
that year. That summer we had a terrific wind and hail storm
which ruined the most of our crops. Lucky for us we carried
hail insurance and collected $2285 for a total loss. This paid
our $2000 cash rent. We did harvest some crop tho. Oats
about 15 bu and corn 20 per A. There was enough grain to
feed out the hogs.

Father and Mother Gist came via train to visit us in September for a month. Father liked to lean on the fence and
watch the hogs. He thought them the finest herd he had ever
seen. Ray took his mother to Sioux City to the fair one day. It
was a wonderful trip for her as she hadn't seen much of this
world while bearing and raising ten children. She yearned for
things to do and see that always seemed to be beyond her
reach. Father Gist was content to as she once put it "sit in a
corner and growl." While the Gist parents were visiting us
Mont and Rena came from Illinois for a few days, driving a
Ford coupe. John and Mathilde thought it the thing to have.

October 20 Fred and Della had another baby, Rena Caroline. I helped the doctor with [the] birth and dressed her in
her first clothes. Mathilde and I took turns staying with them
until Della could be up and around. Ethel Pearl was still in
diapers and used the bottle so we were kept busy with two
babies and the family of nine.

Ray and John decided to dissolve partnership that year so
Ray went to Lyman County [South Dakota] with a real estate
agent, Andrew Christensen, and bought a quarter section of
prairie land for $33 per A[cre]. 20 A. of it was broke[n]. He
paid $875 down on it and rented a quarter two miles away
with buildings for us to live in. We had a sale in January and

divided the proceeds 50–50. Freds went back to Missouri February 1st and John and Mathilde took Fred's job and moved to the Riley farm. They bought a new Ford coupe and some furniture. Mathilde and I were both pregnant.

Mont sent Ray our first radio that fall. It was a Crosley with a horn for the loud speaker. A few radios were beginning to trickle into the country then. We really enjoyed it.[11]

NOTES

1. Interview with Kenneth Helder; Inwood Centennial Book Committee, *Inwood's First 100 Years, 1884–1984* (Dallas: National ShareGraphics, 1984), 66–67.

2. The *Inwood Herald* of June 16, 1921, reports a different version of the wedding celebration. After the regular reception, Olaf Leivestad and Lucille Foote (Ray's and Gladys's future in-laws) "capture[d] the victims" and took them to Raymond and Ethel Brown's (Gladys's sister and her husband) for a reception hosted by the young adults from the local Methodist Church. There, the "crowd pounced upon them and took them from the car." The guests enjoyed refreshments and played outdoor games, and everyone had a "jolly good time." Later, after the newlyweds were safe in their "farm home," "the party swooped down upon them and gave them a friendly chivari."

3. The average size for a farm in Iowa in 1920 was 156.8 acres, just under a quarter section. Most of the acreage on Iowa farms—an average of 134 acres—were "improved." By comparison, when Gladys and Ray moved to South Dakota, the average farm of 464.1 acres included only 243.8 improved acres, probably because of the higher number of ranches in the latter state. Donald B. Dodd and Wynelle S. Dodd, *Historical Statistics of the United States, 1790–1970: Vol. 2. The Midwest* (University: Univ. of Alabama Press, 1976), 12–13; U.S. Department of Agriculture, *Yearbook of Agriculture: 1921* (Washington, D.C.: U.S. Government Printing Office, 1922), 489, 491.

4. Sioux Falls, with a population of 25,202 in 1920, was—and is—the largest city in the Dakotas and is the economic center of southeastern South Dakota, southwestern Minnesota, and northwestern Iowa. Bureau of the Census, *Abstract of the Fourteenth Census of the United States, 1920* (Washington, D.C.: Government Printing Office, 1923), 57.

5. According to Kenneth E. Helder, who belonged to the LTAC from the early days until its demise, it was organized by five young men along the lines of the yet-to-be-founded 4–H clubs. When the men became interested in women, the character of the club changed, and programs were held for both genders on agricultural issues. As the original group scattered and grew older, reunions were held yearly, and then every other year. Once in the late 1940s, recalled Helder, they met on the Gist farm north of Madison.

6. When Agricultural Extension Services were organized at the state and federal levels early in the twentieth century, home extension professionals delivered lectures and held workshops on food preparation, sewing, nutrition, child care, and home management. Dorothy Schwieder, "Education and Change in the Lives of Iowa Farm Women, 1900–1940," *Agricultural History* 60 (Spring 1986): 200–215.

7. The trip from Fairview, South Dakota, to Wheatland, Missouri, on modern roads is about four hundred miles. Driving anywhere, especially in rural areas, was still an adventure in the 1920s. Guidebooks recommended carrying a block and tackle for getting out of mudholes, at least two spare tires, a full set of tools, and flares. One writer advised, "make sure your automobile is fit to fight a long hard battle." By the early 1920s, perhaps six thousand municipal campgrounds—usually located in public parks—had sprung up all over America. They were free, and campers were often provided with privies, electric lights, a central kitchen, a lounge, cold showers, and a laundry room with tubs. Estimates of the number of campers taking advantage of these parks in the mid-1920s ranged from 10 to 12 million. Warren James Belasco, *Americans on the Road: From Autocamp to Motel, 1910–1945* (Cambridge, Mass.: MIT Press, 1979), 30, 71–74.

8. Gladys called her Grandmother McCracken "the world's best grandmother." Minerva served as a nurse to her Ozark neighbors, and learned to write after her children left home so she could correspond with them. She wore no jewelry, kept on wearing old sunbonnets after they went out of style, and dressed only in black—until her funeral when, by her request, she was dressed in white.

9. Between 1919 and 1929, the number of tractors on Great Plains farms more than tripled, from 82,000 to 274,000. Gilbert C. Fite, "Great Plains Farming: A Century of Change and Development," *Agricultural History* 51 (January 1977): 244–256.

10. An unfortunate fondness for alcohol and the death of his wife eventually forced Ray's brother Fred to turn over the care of his children to his siblings. LaMont and Rena took two girls, Rena Caroline and Ethel Pearl, while Ray and Gladys helped Bill, Charles, and "Junior" get on their feet. Charles later died in the Bataan "Death March" after the Japanese capture of the Philippines early in World War II.

11. In 1925, only 10 percent of American homes had radios. By 1935 the percentage was 46, and ten years later two-thirds of all American families could enjoy radio programming. The most popular radio station in southeastern South Dakota in the 1920s was WNAX, which broadcast out of Yankton. Owned by the Gurney Seed & Nursery Company, it employed twenty-seven musicians and broadcast news and weather along with its entertainment programming. Leo Bogart, *The Age of Television: A Study of Viewing Habits and the Impact of Television on American Life* (New York: Frederick Ungar, 1956), 10; Reynold M. Wik, "The Radio in Rural America During the 1920s," *Agricultural History* 55 (October 1981): 344.

RODNEY, KENT, RUTH,
AND THEIR LYMAN COUNTY MENAGERIE,
EARLY 1930s.

MAKING AN HONEST LIVING, 1926–1936

When they migrated to Lyman County, South Dakota, in 1926 the Gists stepped into a different world. Rodney believed his mother went through "culture shock" when she and her family left cozy northwest Iowa for the expansive West. Lyman County, which stretched west from the Missouri River in south-central South Dakota, was still very much a frontier. Settlement of the former Sioux reservation had only begun in 1893; the Milwaukee Road (the Chicago, Milwaukee, St. Paul, and Pacific Railroad) pushed through the previously unfenced cattle range in 1905, barely twenty years before Ray and Gladys pulled up their Iowa roots and transplanted them to West River sod. As recently as 1915, land on the newly opened reservation tracts had been granted to homesteaders through lotteries.

Blue and red tarpaper shacks and more substantial wooden claim shanties still dotted the prairie, relics of the wide-open days of settlement during the West River boom. One Lyman County homesteader described her first view of her new home, which no doubt looked much the same to the Gists in 1926: "As there were no fences or roads—only trails—we lost our way. I shall never forget the utter loneliness which almost overwhelmed me as we drove . . . over the prairie. . . . There was no human habitation—only prairie and sky."[1]

Gladys reveals in her reminiscence a bit of wonder at her pioneer-like existence, but she could not ignore the grim realities. Rainfall was erratic, at best, in the West River country. The great drought of 1909–1915 had ruined thousands of farmers'

dreams and forced half of Stanley County's and over a third of
Perkins County's residents to flee. The soil was hard when dry,
sticky when wet, and always difficult to cultivate. In 1930, the
nearest town, Presho, had a population of 487 souls, who enjoyed neither electricity nor sewage disposal and only limited
medical care; there were no hospitals, four doctors, and only
one dentist in the entire county.[2]

Economic and natural catastrophes of the late 1920s and
1930s threatened even the marginal living the Lyman County
land afforded. The October 1929 stock market crash proved to
be a catalyst for a depression that lingered for more than a
decade. Soft markets had plagued farmers throughout the post–
World War I period, and prices collapsed even further during the
first few years of the depression. Corn dropped from sixty-nine
cents a bushel in 1928 to twenty-seven cents in 1932, and beef
fell from $10.31 per hundredweight to $4.19 and eggs from
twenty-four cents a dozen to a dime. Banks failed at an alarm-
ing rate between 1920 and 1936; two-thirds of South Dakota's
lending institutions closed, and Lyman County lost seven of its
ten banks. Land values in Lyman County plummeted from an
average of thirty-six dollars an acre in 1920 to seventeen dollars
in 1930 and only five dollars in 1940—far below the thirty-three
dollars per acre that Ray paid in 1926. Farm foreclosures in
several representative South Dakota counties quadrupled the
1913–1921 yearly average in 1924 and 1933, and remained double the pre-1921 rate in most of the other depression years.[3]
Deep in the winter of 1934, the *Lyman County Herald* listed
nine "Notice of Mortgage" sales for the week of January 30.

The drought that accompanied the economic slide spawned
dust storms that swept over the plains, scraping off topsoil that
buried fence rows, sifted around windows and doors, and insin-
uated itself into every aspect of people's lives. During one five-
month period in 1934, the state weather bureau reported sixty
separate dust storms. The semi-weekly *Dakota Farmer* exclaimed on May 26, 1934, that "the soil is drifting as never
before—many fences are banked to the top, machinery in fields
and around buildings are covered or nearly so, ditches along
roads are filled and, in places, roadways are drifted as with
snow."

Yet another scourge flourished in the near-desert conditions, as swarms of grasshoppers consumed crops, pasture, and even clothes hanging out to dry. Lyman County suffered from the insects more than most counties. The state extension service reported that at least part, and often all, of the county was "heavily infested" with the hungry insects every year between 1930 and 1935.[4] This certainly would not have surprised Lyman Countians. The 1931 County Fair was canceled because of the extensive crop damage caused by grasshoppers. "Every day," reported the *Herald* on July 16, "you can look up at the sun and see the air full of hoppers, riding on the wind some place and making the sky look like there was an immense snow storm ranging up there. . . . There is many a good working farmer who is going to have to take the count thru the hoppers."

The 'hoppers, the dust, and the crippled economy exacerbated the pioneer conditions the Gists had to endure. Without running water or electricity, and relying on horse power to operate their farm, they lived much as Lyman County settlers had lived twenty or thirty years before. Breakfast sometimes consisted of cooked whole wheat soaked overnight in water. Sunchoking dust storms made lanterns necessary. Wood for fuel came from the dead ash and elm trees along nearby Medicine Creek. One winter Ray bought Gladys a long-wearing winter coat with the bounties he earned for the pelts of skunks he had trapped along the creek, and Gladys made soap from the fat Ray salvaged from the skunks.

Like many other South Dakotans, the Gists also relied on the government to help them through their extended economic crisis. Late in 1934, 39 percent of the state's working population was on relief, including half the state's farmers. In one county in central South Dakota, 80 percent were on relief. Another source of aid for the Gists and virtually all other farm families was the Agricultural Adjustment Administration (AAA) program, which, beginning in 1934, paid benefits to producers who agreed to cut their production of certain commodities.[5]

Despite hard times, the Gist children retained fond memories of the nine years in Lyman County. Rodney and Kent would compete to see who could endure for the longest time the unbearably ticklish sensation of calves licking their toes, and Ruth regularly defeated her older brothers in trying to keep straight faces with mouths full of raw, sour rhubarb. Although a tight budget prevented the family from going into town on most Saturday nights, there were excursions to the annual county fair and once to a circus in Chamberlain. Joining the family was a menagerie of pets, including the Shetland ponies Dolly and Comet, who carried the boys to their one-room schoolhouse a few miles away and raced each other at the Lyman County Fair, a bottle-fed lamb named Petunia, and, a few years later, a not-quite-tame coyote. Gladys managed to find time to take violin lessons from the Methodist minister's wife in Presho. Loyal and generous friends helped the Gists when they needed it, and the family continued to offer support when necessary.

Nevertheless, their time in Lyman County would haunt Ray and Gladys for years. They lost to foreclosure the only land they ever owned. Their government seed and feed loans would remain on the books until after the Second World War. And in 1927 their rented house burned down along with most of their belongings. Gladys and the children were visiting in Iowa at the time, and Ray was left alone at home. One day he heard a thump in the attic. Upon investigating, he found that a ham hanging from the rafters for drying had struck the floor after flames burned through its string. Ray managed to save a few possessions, but the fire destroyed the house and most of what was in it, including Gladys's piano and diamond ring. Five-year-old Kent later helped his parents sift hopelessly through the ashes. They had no insurance.

The fire shattered the Gists' dreams, coming less than two years after their decision to leave comfortable Iowa. Rod called it "a watershed" in Gladys's life, and Ruth believed that Ray "thought he'd finally begun to make a living for his family, and realize a certain amount of success and this destroyed everything." Symbolically, Ray had to replace Gladys's shiny new enamel and chrome Sanico with a rusty old range he found in an abandoned claim shanty. On top of these problems, Gladys's beloved father, Frank Leffler, died in 1934, after a long illness, depriving Gladys and the entire family of the support and guidance they had depended on for years.

It would take Ray and Gladys two decades to recover materially from the fire. They may never have recovered emotionally. One mental scar from these difficult years stemmed from an incident in which a neighbor, observing young Rodney, reported to the county health nurse that the small but healthy toddler was undernourished. Nevertheless, they began to rebuild. As Gladys often said, "We lived through a lot of hard times, but things always seemed to even out." The decade in Lyman County would present the Gists' with their most difficult tests; the evening out would be a long time coming.[6]

1 9 2 6

We traded our red Ford in on a black 1920 model Dodge touring car before we moved west to Presho. The top was the old "surrey" style with side curtains that we could fasten on in inclement and cold weather. The upholstery was of fine black leather. We have not owned a car with such beautiful upholstery since.

On February 22 we moved west to Presho and our new home.[7] The neighbors helped Ray load our things in a railroad emigrant car and Ted went with it.[8]

While they were loading the car I was at Ethel's, miserable with nausea. Kent and Lloyd were playing and Kent stuck his fore finger in the gears of the cream separator and crushed the end of it. We rushed him to a doctor in our car and when I went to turn on [the] hiway two miles west of Inwood Mr. Thorson's car collided with mine and damaged it pretty bad but none of us were hurt. A passing motorist took us to Inwood and Ray had to leave the rail road car loading and get our Dodge to town. It delayed us two or three days. Mr. Thorson paid for fixing [the car] as it was his fault.

Ray bought three cows from our herd sale to take along and went to an auction sale S. W. of Canton in S. Dak. and bought two more holsteins that had been TB tested. We had to get them tested again before we could truck them into Iowa to load and this time they both had it so we shipped them to S[ioux] City as reactors and sold them at a loss. He also bought a collie pup, Jack, for $5.00 to take along.

Our railroad car was loaded with 3 cows, 1 dog, 2 horses, some horse machinery, a dismantled binder, 4 crates of chickens and house furniture.

About a week before moving we had received a letter from [the] L. P. Comps saying they were to be our closest neighbors and inviting us to come to their home until we could get settled. When the railroad car was well on its way we loaded ourselves and the remnants of our things in the Dodge and started west to make our fortune. We got to Comps about 6 P.M. where we received a friendly welcome with strangers and so began a lasting friendship with the first neighbors in our new home and we found many more like them as the years went by.

I was so weak and nauseated from pregnancy that I wasn't able to do much but the rail road car was in Presho so Ray got the stoves and a bed up the next day and we moved in.

It was a little three room house much like "The prairie is my garden" painting by our South Dakota artist Harvey Dunn.[9] We didn't know where to put all the furniture we had brought and it was May before I could fix up the house and do all of my house work.

Ray was really busy. We took 8 or 10 cows of Mr. Comp's to milk. We [were] to have the cream income and he the calves. We had no feed for livestock except what we bought so as soon as grass came I took the car, Kent and the dog and herded the cattle on the prairie near home. I was content and happy and learned to love the beauty of the prairie around me as strength and vitality grew. I hatched some chicks in an incubator we moved with us and a rat caught the most of them in one night.

The shallow well water was unfit for human use so we hauled all our water in barrels and a cream can from an artesian well 2 miles for family use. We kept a can of water in the cave for drinking. We had no mail route so only got mail when we went to Presho 6 miles away about once a week, getting half a dozen daily papers at a time. [*Farm families without refrigeration often used "caves," or root cellars—dug below the frost line—in which to store food. The Gists' cave in Lyman County, Rodney recalled, resembled the storm cellar in* The Wizard of Oz *and was as big as a good-sized closet.*]

In July Ray had an attack of kidney stones. He was in terrible pain and I had to leave him alone while I went after the doctor 6 miles. I drove the Dodge as fast as it would go. The doctor came and gave him morphine and he recovered in a few days.

One evening a car of strangers stopped in. They were a middle aged man and woman and a young woman with a baby. They had been to a celebration in Presho and it had rained until the roads were so sticky with gumbo mud that they could not get home. We fixed them supper, but beds created a problem as we only had one bedroom. We had an extra spring and mattress which we used when needed so I made a bed on the kitchen floor and told the middle-aged couple they could sleep there. She blushed and stammered, "Why we are not married!" They were a jolly group and after breakfast the next morning went on their way.

Rev. Rich and Mrs. Rich called on us in April and she brought me a red geranium. It made a friendly glow, and we accepted an invitation to a welcome party for newcomers at the church.

Mathilde's baby was still born in June in their home near Rock Valley, Iowa. He was a fully developed baby boy, but [the] birth was so long and [as there were] no hospital facilities . . . life was gone when he was born. They buried him in Inwood Cemetery with graveside services. Mathilde's people thought they should have the baby baptized before burial but John thought that foolishness so there was heartache and bitterness over that.

Mathilde wrote that she was coming to take care of me when our baby came so the first of October she came via train. Rodney was born October 4 about 3:30 A.M. Ray had

gone for the doctor when the baby was born so Mathilde and
I were alone and I was surely grateful that she was there.
John came after her in their car and they went to the Black
Hills for a little trip when they left.

This time I had a lovely layette. The LTAC mailed me a
baby shower from Inwood and Mathilde gave me some of her
nice things.

Crops were very poor that year. We cut the grain which
was mostly Russian thistles for hay, and the corn for fodder.
We threshed a little wheat which we kept for seed. We continued to milk Mr. Comp's cows for income.

1 9 2 7

In Feb. we had both of the boys baptized and all joined the
Methodist Church in Presho. Rev. C. D. Arms was pastor
then. It was a friendly church and we attended worship and
S[unday] School there all the years we lived in Lyman County.

In March Uncle Fred McCracken came to visit us and it
seemed a good chance for me to go to Inwood with him to
visit my folks so the boys and I went. [*Fred was Gladys's favorite uncle. A woodworker, leatherworker, and gentle drunk,
Fred was unhappily married and often stayed with Gladys's
mother after Frank Leffler's death. Gladys recalled years later
that Fred was the only reason she had ever allowed a spittoon
in her house.*]

While we were gone, fire started in a defective chimney
on a very windy day and our home with most everything we
had burned to the ground. Ray was there and saved a few
things out of the house, sewing machine, wool rug, a small
desk, one mattress and a few kitchen utensils. I had left my
diamond ring, wrist watch and miscellaneous jewelry at home
because of the baby necessities and washings so all burned

and all other keep sakes. But we were thankful the family were unharmed.

Again [the] Comps opened their home to us until we could find another which took about a week. It was the only year in our lives that we did not have fire insurance. We had neglected to get another policy after moving.[10]

We did not know we had so many friends. The church in Inwood sent us a check for $50 and a box of clothing and household linens. The LTAC of Inwood mailed a kitchen shower and the neighbors and merchants of Presho gave us $150 so we rented another farm known as the Crane place, moved there and somehow got another crop in. We were making installment payments on a cream separator that burned and had to get another, so for the next few months we paid installments on two separators. After that, installment buying for us was an extreme necessity. Some one gave us an old cook stove out of an abandoned house and we salvaged our heater after the fire. It didn't look like much but it worked. The chimney [had fallen] across my beautiful enamel range so it was beyond salvage. I missed it and my piano more than anything. The new home was a larger house, 5 rooms with basement. It was infested with bed bugs so we painted, papered, scrubbed and fought them all year as there were no insecticides then. I don't think there were any bugs when we moved a year later.

There were three sets of farm buildings located on the intersection corners and we all used water from the same artesian well which was across the road north from us. A windmill pumped the water into a big supply tank with an open top. Artesian water comes from the earth warm. It cooled in the big tank so for a cool drink we climbed up a ladder to the top of the tank, dipped a pailful out and carried it across the road home. We had no refrigeration or ice but most homes had a cave which kept things cool, or a cistern in which we suspended pails of milk, butter, etc. on a long rope. For washing and cleaning Ray hauled water across in barrels, put in a few teaspoons of lye and in a few hours the curd settled to the bottom so we could dip out clear soft water. I washed clothes on a wash board thru one big tub of water then boiled the white ones then rinsed through two waters, wringing them by hand. It wasn't as bad as it sounds. We were happy and busy making an honest living. One day when I had finished cleaning up the kitchen after washing I picked up a magazine while I nursed the baby. [T]hese lines flashed across the page: "You can scrub your floor as a dreary drudge, or you can scrub it as queen of your castle." I never forgot the comparison.

We milked 15 cows that summer and lived with cream checks. We raised about enough wheat for seed again and the rest of the crops were mostly cockleburs. Ray fought them in every way that he could but the infestation of the land was overwhelming. There was no weed spray then. We had two brood sows that had big litters of pigs and when they were about two weeks old one sow was dead one morning and we found that cockleburs not only took crops but when young, poisoned animals.

Mother Gist died that year in October and we hired a neighbor girl to stay with me and help with the milking while Ray went to the funeral in Wheatland, Missouri, via train. We sold two of our precious calves to pay expenses.

We heard of a place 2 mi[les East and] ½ [miles] S[outh] of Presho along Medicine Creek being for rent, so Ray wrote to Mr. Albert Hulsether, the owner, who lived in Vashon, Washington. Mr. Hulsether came to visit us and I guess he liked us for he chose us as tenants. It was some of the best farm land in the county but the buildings had been vacant for a year. They were ramshackle and run down and high weeds in all the yards. Mother and Dad Leffler came to visit us in the fall and Mother shook her head and said, "It looks like a wilderness."

1 9 2 8

In January Ray was called to serve on the jury in Kennebec, 9 miles east. [*Kennebec, population 349 in 1930, was the county seat of Lyman County.*] He could easily drive from home but while sitting on a case there came one of the worst blizzards we have ever seen and he was unable to get home for two or three days and nights. No telephones or communications.[11] I got . . . Rodney to sleep and leaving Kent, who was five, in the house with plenty of caution went out early to try to take care of the livestock. Lucky for us the neighbors John and Torv Anderson came over and helped me so we didn't lose any animals. I always was afraid of the horses but was well acquainted with the cattle and milking chores. It turned terribly cold and things started freezing in the cellar so I carried it all about 100 quarts of vegetables and fruit upstairs and sat up most of the night keeping fires. Ray finally made it home and was nearly frantic with worry.

We moved to the Hulsether farm in February. It was a beautiful location with trees along the creek. Mr. Hulsether had the buildings repaired as soon as weather permitted. The house was three old claim shacks moved together making 6 rooms on [the] first floor and one large room upstairs over the south end of the house. It was cold when we moved in, infested by rodents and bed bugs and even a bird's nest in the upstairs room. Mr Hulsether had the two south rooms and upstairs all insulated, replastered and decorated and we papered and painted the other 4 rooms and got rid of the rodents and bed bugs and created a pleasant home. The 4 north rooms which included the kitchen were always cold in winter but we spent 9 happy years here in spite of economic reverses which everybody had in the 1930s. There was plenty of wood along the creek for fuel and we were never very cold but Ray was busy during the winters cutting & sawing by hand.

We started Kent to school that spring when he was only 5. There were only 4 pupils in the country school 2 miles

away. They were all older girls so Kent made the first grade
with plenty of attention. He knew the alphabet, could count,
print and recite innumerable nursery rhymes when he started
to school.

Rodney was 1½ yrs old, a little tow head with rosy cheeks
and learning to talk. We took Kent to school in the car so
Rodney got to go along two trips a day for that and Kent
soon started Rodney's education.

One day I heard Rodney laughing and having a great
time just outside the door. When I looked out there was the
dog Jack tossing a big 4 ft snake around killing it. I was terri-
fied and snatched the baby inside & stripped off his clothes to
examine him for snake bite but I didn't find any. Even a little
garter snake terrifies me; so far I have been able to out run
them.

There was a shallow well of cold soft water here, for
which we were grateful. It all had to be pumped by hand but
there was water in the creek for livestock in spring and summer until it went dry, which usually happened about threshing
time. Then Ray would have to dig a shallow well by hand in
the creek bed and install a pump for livestock. It is amazing
how much water animals can drink when it is being pumped
by hand.

It was a delight to walk along the creek among the trees.
Trees are not common [on the] South Dakota West river prairie. We kept turkeys. The trees and winding creek thru the
pasture made a good natural place for them. There was quite
a lot of running to keep them within the boundary of our
farm, and to outwit a turkey that hides her nest is a real ac-
complishment. It was much to our advantage to find the eggs
before the crows did and exchange a few chicken eggs for her
speckled eggs. We hatched them under R[hode] Island Red
chicken hens, having 10 to 30 hens sitting at a time, then had
the turkeys lay a second clutch of eggs after which a few
would be broody long enough to take the poults when they
hatched. We then turned them loose and they grew up like a
brood of pheasants or quail. In the fall they came home for

food and water and we started fattening them for market. It
was a hit or miss business. We learned never to count profits
until we had it in our pocket but there wasn't much expense
either. One year we raised 325.[12]

The Hulsether farm consisted of 400 A. where we lived,
and 160 A. of prairie hay one mile north. About 200 A. was
under cultivation which Ray farmed with horses.

1 9 2 9

Corn in Lyman County was planted with a lister, one row at
a time and cultivated twice as it grew, with a 2 row cultivator. This year it made about 10 bu. per A. and Ray picked it
all by hand. Wheat made 11 bu. per A. no. 1 quality and bar-
ley 10 per A. light weight. Grain was cut with a horse drawn
binder, shocked and threshed. They were poor crops but we
were thankful for what we had. We milked cows for living
expenses.

The biggest event that year was a deadly disease of our
horses called glanders.[13] Like t[u]b[erculosis] it could be trans-
mitted to humans and we were frightened and aghast when we
discovered what it was. For over a year the horses had been
having a running mucous discharge from the nose and mouth
which kept getting worse. In the summer of 1928 we lost one
work horse that just weakened and died. By spring 1929 we
could see that the other horses were getting it. For awhile we
thought it was distemper and the veterinarian was puzzled as
to diagnosis. Finally he decided to test for glanders and that is
what it proved to be. A few other horses in the community
had it. In the summer of 1927 we [had] hired a neighbor to
cultivate corn and he used one of our bridles giving our horse
infection from his. Because of the nature of the disease the
State ordered all of our horses killed and burned. They had

them appraised and paid us a percentage of the value. We got enough from the 7 head to buy back 4 work horses to continue farming. [*The 1929 account book showed that the horses that died were Queen, Eagle, Croppy, Bill, Topsy, Bird, and Daisy. They were replaced by Pet, Jim, Dolly, and Fronze.*]

To destroy them was one of the hardest things Ray ever had to do. He was always so considerate and kind to his animals that they were like friends. Some of the neighbors offered to help but he said no, that he could handle them better than anyone else and would do it himself if it had to be done, so he led 7 of them out to a straw pile, one by one, shot them and burned them. He set fire to the straw pile and kept adding manure to keep a slow burning fire. Smoke came from the pyre for about three weeks until even the bones were consumed. Then there was the thorough job of disinfecting stables and equipment.

In 1929 the historic crash of the stock market and the ensueing [sic] crash of prices, together with extreme drouth throughout the midwest, was the beginning of a decade of depression. People often speak of these years as the "dirty thirties." Herbert Hoover was President and he became increasingly unpopular as the economic situation of the country grew worse.

When John and Mathilde left Iowa, they went to Mont's in Illinois for a few months then to Wheatland and lived with his folks, or with his father, as Mother Gist died in 1927. In 1926 when we dissolved partnership, John paid off a $300 note on his father's home. By 1929 their money was all gone and they wanted to go to California so insisted on selling his father's place to get their money back. They sold the home taking a 1926 Chevrolet coupe in trade as part payment. Father Gist had no use for a car as he had never owned one and being 80 years old did not want to learn to drive it, so the car was something to resell or pay storage on. They left the car in Wheatland for [their son] Charles to negotiate and brought father Burgess to live with us on their way to California. Charles was pretty unhappy about it but they thought they had fixed things just dandy for father. The farm was a good place where he could be busy and happy. We eventually agreed to pay $250 for the car and a young man coming to work in S. D. brought it to us. We still had the Dodge, but as we couldn't run two cars we stopped buying a license for it and finally made a trailer of the chassis.

We were happy to have father Gist and did everything we could to keep him happy, but he soon got homesick. In October he became acutely ill and we called the doctor for treatment. He became so homesick that he wrote Mont asking him to come get him, so Thanksgiving Mont's family came and took him home with them to Illinois for the winter. In the spring they took him back to Wheatland where he made his home with Charles until his death in 1937.

Dean Brakke started in first grade to school that fall so there were two little boys. He and Kent were great pals for the next 8 years.

1 9 3 0

This was a good crop year and a busy one. We decided that Kent was old enough to ride a pony to school that fall so for his birthday Ray bought him a black Shetland pony. [Kent] had been the world's champion cowboy for about a year and this was a climax of his fondest dreams. He loved "Dolly" from the moment he saw her and never got tired of her. Rodney was now 4 yrs old so we didn't have a baby any more.

In April I got the job of writing census in three townships in Lyman Co. I took Rodney along. We had a farm schedule besides the census count. Because the population and farms were scattered the pay was better than average. I got $1.00 for a farm schedule and ten cents a name. I enjoyed the work and made over $100 which was a big help for us then.[14]

Just before school was out Kent became real sick, and when the doctor came he pronounced it typhoid and pneumonia fever. It was the first serious sickness in the family and we were frightened sick. The doctor came every day for over a week and we nursed according to his instructions day and night, taking turns at the bedside. One evening a car drove in the yard and my Dad got out of it! He said he hadn't been feeling well and rode out with a friend to as he put it to relax and take a vacation. What a comfort! and how happy I was to see him. That night about 3 or 4 A.M. as I sat with Kent I noticed a change in his color and when I put my hand on his forehead it was sticky and clammy with perspiration. In panic I woke Ray and Dad, and Dad, who had nursed a good many people thru pneumonia said, "the fever has broke, and everything is going to be alright now." It seemed to me that all my life when I needed it most, that a few words of encouragement or advice from Dad and things began to straighten out. Kent recovered quickly from that time on. Dad stayed for three weeks. I don't know how much relaxation he got. He enjoyed the creek too. Every day he took the gun and went for a walk among the trees to shoot crows and hunt the turkeys, he said.

In July I became pregnant again and endured the six weeks of extreme nausea. We hired a neighbor girl, Anna Jensen, to stay with us for about a month and do the housework. Her wage was $4 a week, which was current wages for domestic help. After noon dinner dishes were done I told her to rest or do whatever she wanted to do for a couple of hours and she was amazed. She said, "you are the only place I have ever worked where I could do that." She was strong and capable and good help.

In October we took a little trip to visit relatives. We bought a "store" cake and put 4 candles on it to celebrate Rodney's birthday with a picnic dinner on the way the day we left home. We spent the first night with Uncle Fred's near Madison, then on to Milbank, South Dakota, to visit Teds [*Gladys's brother's family*]. Went fishing with them in Big

Stone Lake, then down to Inwood to visit my folks and Raymond's for a few days.

During harvest Bill Gist [*Fred's son*] came looking for work and we decided to keep him so he could go to H[igh] S[chool] that year. His mother was dead and we wanted to help with his education. He helped Ray with the work and rode a horse to Presho to H. School where he was a sophomore. He was an honor student and one of their star basketball players. No boy ever did so well in school with so little money. He finished his last two years of H. S. in Wheatland, Missouri, doing any kind of work that he could find, and graduated with honors.

1 9 3 1

Ruth was born March 16. By daylight I knew the time had come, so the men hurried chores and Ray took Rodney to visit school with Kent, and sent Bill for the Dr. Newman when he went to Presho to H. S. The doctor was prompt, as he remembered he hadn't hurried much when Rodney was born. We were alone with the doctor. He was a very capable obstetrician, his babies numbered in the thousands. Ray administered the anesthetic. I was utterly exhausted from the birth, but when I heard Ray say, "Mamma it's a little girl!" I thought she was well worth it. They took care of us, then Ray made some coffee. I guess they needed a coffee break, especially Ray. He went after Rodney at noon and told him about the new baby on the way home. Rodney came dashing into the bedroom with his big blue eyes shining.

"Where did we get him?"

"God gave her to us."

"Did He make the calves and pigs and chickens?"

"Yes, He makes all little babies."

"Gee, He sure has been busy around here lately hasn't He?"

Perhaps we did not discuss sex matters enough with our children but now I believe that it is grossly overdone. I believe that they should be taught the fundamentals of procreation, but that mystery is part of the charm of sex until it finds fulfillment in marriage and love. In my lifetime it has been removed from marriage and dissected, discussed, psychoanalyzed and spelled out, often in lurid form on thousands of printed pages, and pictured on our magic screens in all sorts of suggestive manner until it is no wonder so many of our people are submerged and seemingly uncapable of any self control. Our federal, State and local welfare agencies are frantically trying to stem the tide of illegitimacy and its ever growing demands for public support.

Our Chevy coupe was too small for our growing family, there were six of us with Bill, so we traded it for a 1928 Chevy sedan and financed it thru a finance co[mpany]. We really had a hard time getting it paid for.[15]

Periodically we had our cattle tested for T. B. and in April that year three of our milk cows tested to have it so we sold them as reactors and bought two for replacement.

This was the first grasshopper year, the beginning of bare earth farming.

After World War One the Gov't issued a paid up life insurance policy to all of the veterans based on their service. Ray's amounted to $1501. [In t]he spring of 1931 a bill was passed to pay these policies in two cash payments. We received the first $750 in April.[16] We bought a new Maytag washing machine that ran with a gas motor so I hung up my washboard. We used the machine for our family washings for 25 years.

Ray went to an auction sale and bought five beautiful Poland China purebred sows for $155. They had good litters but that year prices dropped and we sold the five sows in September for $63.87 and were forced to sell the pigs because of no feed for $3.50 each and $3.10 per cut.

The grasshoppers hatched in June and the earth was alive
with them. As they grew the crops disappeared, alfalfa and
tender grass, then when the grain headed out they cut it off
just below the head. There was one or more on every stalk.
From the grain they invaded the corn fields and soon there
was nothing left but a dry stump of the stalk. Even the leaves
of the trees were stripped and by September the earth was
bare, hot and dry. Farmers frantically tried poisoning, spread-
ing it in bran with the grain seeders. There were so many piled
dead in our potato patch that they stank but we did not save
the spuds. In August the temperature ran over 100 [degrees]
every day and [the grasshoppers] sat on the shady side of anything they could find, the buildings, fence posts etc., spaced
evenly apart, all at the same angle, like an army formation.
[*Gladys wrote in her account book that despite her efforts to
keep the potato plants green, they never blossomed and the
only potato harvest was a bushel of spuds the size of marbles.
The entire garden yielded nothing in 1931 — "not one meal of
anything."*]
We had a Sunday School picnic in the trees along the
creek before shade was completely gone. I was holding Ruth
on my lap leisurely visiting when she suddenly started scream-
ing with pain. We found a round hole on her little bald head
about the size of a pin head. Mr G[rass]Hopper had taken a
nip. We soon learned not to hang any rayon, nylon or
starched clothing on the line. It was a hazard to wear rayon
hose while driving the car. We tried to keep them out of the
houses but they found various ways of getting in, even coming
down the chimneys. I removed the starched curtains and the
shades became unevenly scalloped along the edges.

1 9 3 2

The year that such a disaster strikes a farming community is not so bad as the years of recovery. Feed was very scarce. We borrowed a $250 feed loan from the Gov't to winter our livestock and in the spring another loan for seed. It took us fifteen years to pay all the money back, struggling under the burdens of the debts of the 1930s.[17] 1932 was a struggle to keep going. It was dry but we raised some crops for feed and seed. Grain made about 10 bu. per A. Egg prices fell to $.06 per dozen and butter fat $.12 a lb.[18]

One of our friends, John Byker, who went to Lyman County the year we did, gave up in April and went back to Rock Valley, Iowa, to find work. They had 8 children and had fought cold and hunger all winter.[19] Eight of their cows which was the source of their living had died of starvation. There was no market for hogs, so he brought his 17 pigs to our yard and unloaded them. We didn't want them either as we had little feed, no market, and the Gov't was advocating killing little pigs to reduce the surplus.[20] We kept them until fall and sold them with ours at an average price of $3.54 per head.

In July, some of the neighbors began to lose cattle with anthrax. We promptly had ours vaccinated and in about a week, while Ray was gone threshing, the boys went after the cows one evening and found "old Roany" dead by a water hole. We knew what it was, but as they had been vaccinated we felt quite helpless. A day or two later when we went to milk one morning the bull was lying by the barn dead and one milk cow, busy chewing her cud, was obviously about to drop. We lost five altogether. It seemed to strike the healthiest ones. We learned that the only way to know if they had it before they just dropped dead was to take their temperature with a fever thermometer. A cow's natural temperature is 102–104 [degrees]. We put them all in the stanchion and took their temperature every night with a rectal thermometer. If it was over 104 we got the veterinarian to give them a serum to counteract the disease. In this way we saved any further loss but we had a big veterinarian bill.

Anthrax is communicable to other animals and also to man. The germs are known to live in the soil for years and still be potent so it is important to dispose of the dead animals with extreme care wherever they drop if possible, so again, Ray kept slow burning pyres for three weeks. The weather was extremely hot and we were beset with work and worry. One evening I noticed Rodney seemed ill, and his temperature registered 103. We rushed him to the doctor sick with fright but the doctor assured us it was not anthrax. It made us realize that we had better give thanks for the health of our family and count our blessings.

That year we spent $141.16 for groceries besides our farm produce, and $31.75 for clothing. We had wood fuel. We did not go hungry and I "made over" warm clothes for the children, even mittens. We weren't style models, but not uncomfortable and better off than many others. [*Gladys recorded only two $.75 expenditures for "entertainment" for all of 1932.*]

Ray had bred his mares to raise colts that year, including Dolly. Rodney would soon be old enough for school and would need a pony to ride. Dolly didn't show much evidence of becoming a mother so Ray had about decided there wasn't going to be a Shetland. On May 30 he went to the barn as usual as soon as he was up and dressed, and I saw him come striding back. The little colt was there! The children weren't up yet so I rushed out with him to see it. She was a cute little thing, about the size of a big dog, wobbling around in a dazed sort of way. I went back in to prepare breakfast and decided to let the boys find it. At our house everybody got up and dressed before breakfast and we ate all of our meals around the table together. Ray once remarked that we had a talker, a singer and a giggler for entertainment. Some meals were hurried when they were in school, but they were nearly always happy. Kent was usually the first one up, and soon came bursting back to the kitchen with the great news. He woke Rodney and the baby and we all went to the barn to adore the newcomer. They named her Comet, and she was Rodney's pony.

They had a succession of dogs, cats, rabbits, lambs, chickens, and goats as the years went by, but their ponies were their greatest pets. Comet became tame, and a perfect child's pony. That summer they spent hours playing with her, dressing her in their coats and hats and imaginations ran wild. The boys learned a lot from their ponies. To learn to ride was their first big challenge in life. It was something they had to do alone. We could help them on and give them the reins and then they were on their own. Of course they fell off a few times, but learned tenacity to get up and try again, each time a little wiser. They learned the futility of frustrated bawling. It's better to use your head to figure the best way out of your dilemma. They learned to give comfort and kindness to their pets in order to receive the same from them, and most of all there was the love and pride of a boy for something of his own to use and care for. They always celebrated Comet's birthday with an extra helping of feed and once there was a mud cake with succulent green topping.

We still owed Mr. Hulsether for our 1931 cash rent and when Ray sent him a small payment he wrote back and said the debt was cancelled. If the land didn't produce anything we need not pay for it. He was a very considerate landlord. We farmed his place for nine years.

Uncle Bob Torrey loaned us $50 in August so we wouldn't lose our car. When we sold our turkeys in December we sent it back to him with interest. He promptly returned the interest.[21]

Some friends, Mr. & Mrs. Zee Ritchie and family gave up farming in Lyman County that fall and moved to Omaha. They offered to sell us their piano for $25. We managed to scare up the money to buy it and it was a very happy day for me when it was moved into our living room. The children and I sang a lot as they grew up and now we could have some music to go with our voices.

1 9 3 3

In 1933 prices hit bottom. We put in another crop, hoping, but grasshoppers came again and ate it about as fast as it came up. Ray mowed what he could of the grain for hay. All corn was eaten to the bare ground and he got 5 or 6 loads of cane for feed. We kept 25 turkey hens and sold about $350 of turkeys that fall which was the biggest income we had from the farm. We refinanced our feed loan and paid a little on it by selling our stock down to a minimum.[22] We also paid the most of our cash rent.

That year the Gov't started building dams to conserve, thus giving men work. Ray worked with 4 horses and fresno [*an earth-moving device that operated something like a combination of a grader and a wheelbarrow*] part of the time to get money to live. I fixed his noon lunch and he worked ten hours a day.

We kept the boys in school. They rode their ponies two miles to the country school. They each had a "book satchel" which hung by a strap from the shoulder and they carried their noon lunch and school supplies in that.

Our food was not fancy, but nourishing. We cooked whole wheat grain for cereal, sometimes had it ground. Also had corn ground in Presho for meal. I made my own yeast and baked bread and we had our dairy and poultry products and meat. We rationed our money for necessities and allowed a mimimum for gasoline. The Grocer complained that so many people spent their money at the gas stations and charged their groceries. We paid cash for groceries first. In all our married years we have never run a grocery bill except perhaps for two or three weeks during siege of harvest, then it was promptly paid.

1 9 3 4

1934 was one of the worst years for me. It was the year of the
great dust storms. By mid-summer the farms were a barren desert. Each day at sunrise the wind came up and the air was
filled with blowing cutting soil. It was like a desert sand
storm. Many days visibility was so poor that the cars on the
road were driven with lights on. Dirt drifted along the fences
or other obstructions, piling up like snow drifts.

I kept the food in the cave and in tight containers but we
breathed and ate dust all day. Each evening the sun set red
and the wind died down and settled into a cooling peace, only
to begin again the next day. In the mornings I wiped a thick
layer of dust off of the tables and dishes before serving breakfast and each evening we washed in cool water trying to re-
fresh ourselves for sleep. Ray worked long hard days on a
Gov't project along with our neighbors to get money to live
on. We managed to raise our own meat and keep 8 milk cows,
buying feed for them. There was no market for livestock. The
Gov't paid us $156 for ten head of cattle and sent them south
to people who had pasture.[23]

Ray cut our corn, when it was about knee high, for fodder and got about 7 loads. This was the only crop of any kind
that we raised. We lost two of our work horses that year.
There is an area of land in Lyman County that they called
alkali soil. When hay or grain raised on it, especially in dry
years, was fed to livestock they lost all their hair and their
hooves came off. We happened to buy some of that feed and
one of our horses, "old Jim," became alkalied and died. I
[had] bought 30 hatching eggs from a lady while writing census in that area in 1930 and when they hatched the chicks'
down never seemed to dry and they all died when two or three
days old.

Dolly had another colt which they named Pesty and Kent
traded him to Raymond for a lamb. When his lamb was
about grown it got into some cracked wheat feed and found-

ered and died. We pulled the wool off of it and Mother Leffler and I washed and carded it and put it in a quilt. It made a soft warm interlining.

My father's health was gradually getting worse. He became paralyzed and in a wheel chair from high blood pressure and his mind was also failing. We made three trips to Inwood that year to help care for him and comfort Mother. We went in April and again in September, but had just been home a few days when I was called back. Ray took me and returned home the next day to keep the boys in school and I kept Ruth who was then 3 years old and stayed 3 weeks to help care for him until he passed away on October 4th. There was a special bond of affection between my father and I. His suffering and death removed a very real pillar of strength from my life.

Our land lord, Mr. Hulsether, did not lose faith in Lyman County. He decided to build a new barn for the livestock which was badly needed. Ray helped the carpenter build it and in this way paid our back cash rent and earned some money besides. By this time nearly every one was dependent on Gov't projects and aid.

We refinanced our loans and kept as self-supporting as possible.

1 9 3 5

W started this year about $500 in debt. We had managed to keep enough horses to farm with and our 8 milk cows. Feeding them was a never ending problem. We only had two pigs which we butchered for meat. We had a few hens and turkeys for breeders. We managed to get enough seed to farm the land and raised 660 bu. of wheat, 1180 bu. oats and 600 bu. corn. For this we were very thankful as it at least was enough to carry on.

In summer we milked our cows in the barn yard. Just took the pail and a one legged stool and sat down and milked. If the cow moved, we did too. One evening while we were milking, a black rain cloud with sharp lightening and thunder appeared in the sky. We watched it with a prayer in our hearts for a down pour. It began to sprinkle and we dashed under a shed roof for shelter. It was only a light shower and when we emerged the dusty ground was just mottled with rain drops. The most brilliant rainbow that I have ever seen spanned the sky in the east. It was a double one. I walked to the corner of the cow lot and stood with my milk pail and stool just looking at it, sick with disappointment. I wished I was at the end of it or anyplace but where I was. My mind flew back across the years to when I was a little girl. I had gone with my parents to visit a neighbor who had a little boy about my age named Dewey Porter Thatch. Dewey was lucky, he had Granny.

Granny was one of the most colorful characters I have ever known. She had a room of her own, furnished with a bed covered with a straw tick, feather bed and patch work quilts. Woe be unto anyone who sat on her bed. There was a stand table with a few knick knacks and pill bottles on it, and a low wooden rocker. Granny was nearly always in her rocker smoking a clay pipe, and she had a tobacco juiced cuspidor conveniently by her side on the floor. This I carefully stepped around. Granny had the wisdom of the aged, and she could keep us spell bound with wonderful stories. She also knew how to get rid of us when she got tired of us.

On this afternoon, we dashed into her room to find sanctuary from a rain shower, then back again later to tell her of the beautiful rainbow. Now a rainbow was a thing of wonder, and the most amazing thing about one was the pot of gold at the end of it. We could see the end of it on a rocky hill just east of the house in the pasture so we hunted up a gunny sack and set out. By the time we got to the top of the hill the rainbow was gone, but there was a large flat rock that was splintered out in all directions like an asterisk. This must be gold!

We took some of it back to Granny who promised to find out for sure, and then it was time for me to go home.

Here I was again, years later, looking at a rainbow, and the brilliant colors shone across the rain-wet leaves of the trees along the creek and pointed right to my feet. Suddenly I knew that the rocks of faith and hope and love are much more precious than a pot of gold. These things I had, and I meant to keep them, right where I was.

1 9 3 6

We started the year even deeper in debt, but the cows were bringing a better income and we had more poultry and feed on hand to continue farming.[24]

My mother who was living in an apartment in Inwood was becoming increasingly lonely and "nerve sick" since father's death and we thought perhaps a change, and something of her own to work for would be good therapy. She loved to be out doors so we invited her to spend the summer with us and we would fix a place for her to raise 100 chicks, and we would give her a share of turkey profits if she helped find the eggs and hatch them. She came in May and for awhile things went fine, but by July she was so beset with nerves and the heat she insisted on going back to Inwood to be near her Doctor. That fall Ted came out and hauled her chickens to market and we sent her a check for $20 turkey money so she could spend the winter in California with Ira who was living in Los Angeles. She really enjoyed the winter there and spent 6 months with them.

In May 1936 Dolly, Kent's pony, died with old age. She must have been 25–30 years old. We had a veterinarian to treat her but there was nothing he could do. Kent cared for her and was heart broken when she died.

In February Ray was cleaning ashes from the old cook stove one morning and the bottom was so rusted that sparks fell on the floor. We promptly moved it out of the house and got along with a heater and an old kerosene stove until we finally sent to Sears Roebuck for a new range, buying it on the installment plan. We paid for it during that year. It was a beautiful ivory and sea green enamel range built on boxlike lines and we used it for many years. I enjoyed using it and keeping the highly polished steel top clean and shining.

This was another bad year as the grasshoppers came again and destroyed all crops except for a little rough feed.

The Gov't paid World War One vets the last half of their insurance policies so with the $750 Ray paid some bills and got our finances in the best order we could and rented an 80 A. farm from Mrs. Bert Clark in eastern South Dakota near Canton[25] and we prepared to move from Lyman County where we had struggled for eleven years against the great economic depression of the 1930's combined with some of the most devastating forces of nature.

It was not all bad. We were bles[sed] with good health and a zest for daily living. We cherished the things that we had, and were happy in spite of reverses. Our children grew and waxed strong, both in stature and in character. As I look back now (in 1960) I remember only the good times that we had, and the many friends we made. The Ladies Aid of the church gave me a handkerchief shower before we left, and the school parties and farewell dinners were heart warming as they bade us God speed and helped us off to our new home.

N O T E S

1. Paula M. Nelson, *After the West Was Won: Homesteaders and Town-Builders in Western South Dakota, 1900–1917* (Iowa City: Univ. of Iowa Press, 1986), 17–19, 26, 30. See also *South Dakota: Fifty Years of Progress, 1889–1939* (Sioux Falls: South Dakota Golden Anniversary Book Co., 1939), 96–97.

2. Nelson, *After the West Was Won,* 11–12, 122–130; Bureau of the Census, *Fifteenth Census of the United States, 1930: Vol. 1. Population* (Washington, D.C.: U.S. Government Printing Office, 1931), 1026; W. F. Kumlien, "The

Rural Health Situation in South Dakota," Bulletin 258 (Brookings: Agricultural Experiment Station, South Dakota State College, 1931), 19, 21.

3. T. Hillard Cox and L. M. Brown, "South Dakota Farm Prices, 1890–1937," Bulletin 317 (Brookings: Agricultural Experiment Station, South Dakota State College, 1938); Gabriel Lundy, "Farm Mortgage Experience in South Dakota, 1910–1940," Bulletin 370 (Brookings: Agricultural Experiment Station, South Dakota State College, 1943), 11; Thomas J. Pressley and William H. Scofield, *Farm Real Estate Values in the United States by Counties, 1850–1959* (Seattle: Univ. of Washington Press, 1965), 38; W. F. Kumlien, "A Graphic Summary of the Relief Situation in South Dakota, 1930–1935," Bulletin 310 (Brookings: Agricultural Experiment Station, South Dakota State College, 1934), 15.

4. Kumlien, "A Graphic Summary," 40–43.

5. Herbert Schell, *History of South Dakota*, 3d ed. (Lincoln: Univ. of Nebraska Press, 1975), 292; D. Jerome Tweton, *The New Deal at the Grass Roots: Programs for the People in Otter Tail County, Minnesota* (St. Paul: Minnesota Historical Society Press, 1988), 114–33. Ray earned $274.80 from the Civil Works Administration in 1934; he bought grain and hay for feed with "CWA Scrip." Ray also accepted $177.66 from the hog, wheat, and corn-hog programs of the AAA. In 1935 he received $61.85 in government allotment checks, and the next year he received $37.54 for cutting his wheat production, plus $86.64 under a federal soil erosion program.

6. The depression years have naturally sparked a lot of interest in the experiences of farm families. For a brief look at the problems and responses of women in Boone County, Nebraska, and Lyman County, South Dakota, see Dorothy Schwieder and Deborah Fink, "Plains Women: Rural Life in the 1930s," *Great Plains Quarterly* 8 (Spring 1988): 79–88. For a detailed, nearly daily account of Iowa farm life in the depths of the depression, see H. Roger Grant and L. Edward Purcell, eds., *Years of Struggle: The Farm Diary of Elmer G. Powers, 1931–1936* (Ames: Iowa State Univ. Press, 1976). The experiences during the 1920s and 1930s of a North Dakota woman a little younger than Gladys can be found in Ann Marie Low's *Dust Bowl Diary* (Lincoln: Univ. of Nebraska Press, 1984), a heavily edited and annotated version of a diary that Low kept during the period.

7. The LTAC honored the Gists with a skating party and an oyster supper, and the *Inwood Herald,* in reporting their departure, February 4 and 25, 1926 "wished[ed] them every success in the new country."

8. "Immigrant cars" had for years transported settlers and their personal property to the west. Originally, they were boxcars in which livestock, household goods, and families all rode together. For descriptions of late-nineteenth century immigrant cars, see John Vogel, "Great Lakes Lumber on the Great Plains: Laird, Norton Lumber company in South Dakota" (Ph.D. diss., Marquette University, 1989), 48.

9. Harvey Dunn (1884–1952) was a South Dakota-reared student of Howard Pyle and a popular magazine illustrator, whose most famous painting, "The Prairie is My Garden"—actually named "This, My Garden" by the artist—portrays a woman and her two daughters gathering wildflowers from the windswept Dakota prairie with a primitive homestead in the background. For a brief,

illustrated biography of Dunn, see Robert F. Karolevitz, *The Prairie Is My Garden: The Story of Harvey Dunn, Artist* (Aberdeen, S.Dak.: North Plains Press, 1969).

10. The Gists' 1931 account book records a $15.75 payment for fire insurance.

11. As late as 1930, well under half (42.9 percent) of South Dakotans in three representative counties had the use of telephones. By 1934, the proportion had dropped to 32.3 percent, according to Paul H. Landis, *Rural Relief in South Dakota* (Brookings: Agricultural Experiment Station, South Dakota State College, 1934), 49.

12. In 1928, the Gists' turkey income was $72.56. In other years, profits ranged from $25 to over $100. Turkeys could provide a significant portion of the families' income; in 1931, when turkeys brought in nearly $126, their income from livestock, eggs, and cream (there were no crops that year) totaled only $1,063.72.

13. Glanders was a highly contagious disease among horses, mules, goats, sheep, and even humans. It caused a hardening of the glands, and ulceration of mucous membranes, resulting in a sticky discharge. According to the U.S. Department of Agriculture's *Yearbook* for 1933, (Washington, D.C.: U.S. Government Printing Office, 1933), 232, glanders, "once common in many sections of the United States," had "become rare."

14. Although it is now impossible to tell in which townships Gladys worked, Presho township, where the Gists lived, had a population of 165 in 1930 (*Fifteenth Census of the United States*, 1016). Gladys recorded an exact figure of $111.40 in earnings for conducting the census.

15. The loan from the General Motors Corporation was paid off in 1932.

16. It is unclear whether this payment was related to the controversial War World I veterans' bonus, which by the early 1930s many veterans believed should be paid early. A "Bonus Army" marched on Washington in 1932, but the "Bonus Bill" failed to pass the Senate, and the "Army" was dispersed by units from the regular Army. A bonus bill finally was passed in 1936, over Franklin Roosevelt's veto. It paid out $2 billion to veterans in 1936 rather than on the originally scheduled date in 1945. See Frederick Lewis Allen, *Since Yesterday: The 1930s in America* (New York: Harper and Row/Perennial Library, 1940), 66–68; Arthur S. Schlesinger, Jr., *The Politics of Upheaval* (Boston: Houghton Mifflin, 1960), 504.

17. The Federal government lent money to buy seed and other operational necessities eight of the years between 1921 and 1932, and in 1932–1933 the first state and federal feed loans were made. The Gists eventually paid back $1,964.08 to the federal government and to the companies through which they refinanced at least one of their loans; the last payment was made in 1946. For further information, see Tweton, *The New Deal at the Grass Roots*, 125–26.

18. According to Gladys's records, egg prices in 1931 had generally ranged between $.09 and $.14½ per dozen, with two shipments late in the year going for $.18 and $.20. Cream usually brought $.18 to $.28 per pound.

19. Between 1930 and 1935 Lyman County lost 9.7 percent of its population. See Kumlien, "A Graphic Summary," 53.

20. In 1933, as part of its surplus-eradication program, the federal government, through the Agricultural Adjustment Administration, directed cotton farmers to plow under part of their crops and hog farmers to kill young pigs and pregnant sows (whose carcasses would be used for food and fertilizer) in return for benefit payments. See Gilbert C. Fite, *American Farmers: The New Minority,* (Bloomington: Indiana Univ. Press, 1981) 56.

21. Ray's Uncle Robert Torrey worked in a bank in Los Angeles. He and his wife had no children but raised a girl named Anna.

22. The Gists owed $304 on their feed loan by September 1932, plus $8.82 in interest. They had also taken out a $200 federal seed loan. On May 1, they took out another $400 loan and used it and $95.89 of cattle and hog income to pay off the initial feed loan and $50 of the seed loan.

23. A federal program to buy up cattle in parts of twenty-five of the hardest-hit drought states was organized in the summer of 1934. Excess cattle were bought and sent to other, greener pastures, destroyed, or distributed as meat to families on relief. The government eventually purchased nearly nine million cattle. Roger Lambert, "New Deal Experiences in Production Control: The Livestock Program, 1933–1935" (Ph.D. diss., Univ. of Oklahoma, 1962), 149–216.

24. The Gists began the year $1,328 in debt, including $1,000 in government loans and $78 in back rent.

25. Lincoln County farms averaged only 195.8 acres apiece, compared to 1,143.6 acres in Lyman County in 1940, according to the Bureau of the Census, *Census of Agriculture, 1940–South Dakota* (Washington, D.C.: U.S. Government Printing Office, 1942), 470–71.

RODNEY, EDITH, KENT, AND GLADYS,
SITTING ON THE BUMPER OF THE 1929 CHEVY
THEY BOUGHT IN 1932.

A FULL LIFE, 1937–1945

The depression drove the Gists back to their roots, to a small farm west of Canton, South Dakota, just across the Big Sioux River from Inwood, Iowa. According to census figures, Canton, the seat of Lincoln County, had a population of 2,270 in 1930. The failed pioneers found it difficult to settle in. No sooner had they unloaded their household into the latest in a string of rented homes than the sheriff of Lincoln County "came calling," according to Kent, "to inform Dad that they did not need anyone else on relief in Lincoln County." In one of the few public displays of anger his children witnessed, Ray "informed the [sheriff] that he had not requested any help, and was not likely to do so, and to kindly get the hell out and not come back."

Although they attended the United Methodist Church in Canton for a time, they felt out of place in their well-worn clothes and soon switched to a Congregational Church in Worthing, a village of 262 people northwest of Canton. Kent, who had begun high school in Presho, suffered through a few tough months at Canton High School, then happily finished his junior and senior years in Worthing.

This lowest period in the Gists' lives ended in early 1940 when they moved to a farm near Madison in Lake County, about eighty miles northwest of Canton. Madison, the county seat, with a population of just over 5,000 in 1940, was the commercial center for a number of southeastern South Dakota counties and had a two-year teachers' college.[1] Although they would rent several different farms over the next quarter century,

Ray and Gladys would never again undertake a major move. Here their children would become adults, and here they would finally find prosperity. In many ways, they would finally enter the twentieth century in Lake County, as their farming methods and lifestyles were irrevocably altered by growing abundance and modern technology.

Another constant in their lives during this period was the presence of Gladys's mother Rhodemia. The death of her husband in 1934, as well as her own health problems, forced "Demia" to live with her children much of the time from the late 1930s until her own death in 1951. Reluctant to leave the familiar confines of northwest Iowa, she nevertheless lived with Ray and Gladys on and off for well over a decade, joining a long line of parents, nephews, and siblings who stayed with the family for extended periods. In fact, late in her life Gladys suggested to Ruth that one reason Ray had moved all the way to Presho in 1926 was to escape from his relatives.

With the Gists, Rhodemia had her own room upstairs. Ruth and Rod remembered her as a kind, if a little peculiar, grandmother who sometimes undertook small projects with them. She was always sick. Rod believed that she "enjoyed ill-health" and suspected that doctors—to whom she was devoted—often prescribed placebos to treat her hypochondria. Both Rod and Ruth recalled Grandma Leffler occasionally calling them into her room before they left for school to solemnly tell them goodbye; she assured them she would be dead before they returned. Rod's ambition to be a doctor, not surprisingly, earned him a special place in her heart.

Of course, the Second World War had a huge impact on the Gists. Kent echoed contemporaries and historians alike when he wrote four decades later that "nothing would ever be the same again." Ray and Gladys and their offspring contributed to the war effort in the same ways as millions of other Americans did: they bought war bonds, rolled bandages, produced food for the troops—and Kent and Rod both served in the war's Pacific theater.

Although war had been raging in Europe for two years, Lake Countians were as surprised as any other Americans at the Japanese attack on Pearl Harbor in December 1941. On December 6, the day before the "day that will live in infamy," the

Madison Daily Leader reported unseasonably balmly weather
with highs in the 30s and reminded Christmas shoppers that they
should get an early start, because stepped-up defense production
would force cutbacks in civilian consumption. The *Daily Leader*
also urged readers to buy defense bonds, foreshadowing the
huge bond drives during the war. Otherwise, life went on as
usual, as the Lyric Theater advertised Ronald Reagan in the
motion picture *Nine Lives Are Not Enough* in the same issue of
the newspaper, and various local organizations announced their
Christmas parties.

Suddenly the United States was at war. The *Daily Leader*
continued to count down the shopping days until Christmas, but
maps of exotic Pacific battlefields began to appear, and news of
Lake County's first war dead, a sailor from Wentworth, was
announced in the paper two days before Christmas. "War fanat-
icism" struck the city at about the same time, when a group of
women complained to the Chamber of Commerce about the
local sale of Christmas decorations manufactured in Japan.
Other issues over the next couple of years (August 15, 1942, and
April 22, 1943) announced the onset of tire rationing, described
air raid procedures, applauded the county's purchase of almost
$200,000 in war bonds in early 1943, and printed a nearly daily
column of news about the scores of Lake County men entering
the service.

Ray and Gladys's sons succeeded hundreds of ancestors
who had fought in 200 years of American wars. Kent left for the
Army on Easter Sunday, 1943, after undergoing training for the
Signal Corps. Rod departed in February 1945, just a few
months after his eighteenth birthday. Kent would spend more
than two-and-a-half years in the service and see duty at several
posts in the Pacific. Rod remained in the Army for twenty-one
months, and would be en route to the western Pacific when
Japan surrendered, ending the war.

The Gist boys joined the melting pot of American boys
brought together to fight Fascism and Japanese expansionism.
They traveled all over the country from induction centers to
training camps to staging areas. They befriended boys and men
from every part of the United States; witnessed far more drunk-
enness and gambling then they had ever seen in rural South
Dakota. Like soldiers of all ages, they saw the best and worst

that humankind had to offer. Rod's first letter home, dated February 19, 1945, after he had actually been in the Army for less than half-a-day and had yet to leave the reception center at Fort Snelling in St. Paul, overflowed with youthful enthusiasm over his experiences. The fellows he had met so far were "mighty swell," the food was "really swell," and he was "in the best of spirits." He closed with a summary of the wartime experiences of millions of young men: "Boy I've seen and done enough to write a book. There's so much to write about I don't know where to begin."

Gladys filed away all of Rod's weekly letters home, carefully recording on its envelope the date he had written each letter. They currently are stored in a hand-painted wooden box given to Rod by a Japanese prisoner of war in Manila. Most of Kent's letters were unavailable, but he provided a detailed memoir of his wartime experience, from which much of the following is drawn.

Rod frequently described the terrain, weather, and crops he viewed from the troop trains that carried him from post to post. A common complaint in the letters was that he seemed to be tired all the time, and he reported that he actually slept through a mock attack during maneuvers. Chatty commentary about machine gun "kill ratios" and church services appear alongside each other. Germany surrendered while Rod was at Camp Hood, Texas, and by the time he completed his training, the atomic bomb had, for all intents and purposes, ended the war with Japan. Nevertheless, he soon found himself in the Philippines for more than a year, where his primary duty was helping to manage an officers' club. He celebrated his nineteenth birthday at the Manila Symphony Orchestra, learned to work with Filipino laborers and Japanese prisoners of war, toured the famous fortifications at Corregidor, and often ended his letters with phrases written in Spanish and Tagalog.

Kent also passed through Fort Snelling early in his military career, but his and Rod's experiences in the Army were otherwise very different. The elder Gist son trained in California, took a cross-country train to New Jersey, then passed through the Panama Canal—"an exciting experience for a South Dakota boy"—on the way to the South Pacific. The journey lasted thirty-three days, and Kent complained that "the food on the USS John

Lykes was not like Mother used to cook. It wasn't even like the army cooks at Camp Kohler used to cook."

He was shuffled around the western Pacific, from New Caledonia to Guadalcanal to Iwo Jima, where he saw the flag flying from Mt. Suribachi as soon as the Marines raised it. As a signalman assigned to the Air Corps to encode and decode messages regarding air traffic, Kent never fired a gun in anger, but in a V-Mail letter dated March 3, 1945, he tried to convince his parents that he was still safe, despite being in the middle of a battle zone in which 6,800 American soldiers and sailors died. "I guess maybe you would like to . . . read a few words as put down by the hand that has trembled on Iwo Jima," he began. "We dig our holes deep here, with no urging," he quickly assured Ray and Gladys. "Not being a front line outfit, I'll probably continue to be OK."

Both young men experienced places, people, and responsibilities that expanded their horizons and changed their lives. The war, perhaps more than anything else, created a transition between generations, at least in terms of experiences and expectations. By the same token, the war also permanently changed the lives of family members left at home, where the prosperity spawned by the war allowed the Gists and thousands of other farm families to finally achieve economic success.[2] In the end, this worldwide catastrophe would be the most important thing that ever happened to the Gists.

1 9 3 7

The winter weather of 1936–37 was one of the worst that we have seen. The snow came early and drifts as high as houses piled up.

We spent the winter getting ready to move, trying to sell some of the things we had and get money to move with. Packing and sorting and planning. Ted and Edith were moving from Inwood to California and wanted to dispose of their piano so we sold ours for $20 and bought theirs for $25.

On March 4 we hired 4 regular stock trucks and loaded our car and trailer and moved to a farm 6 miles west, 1¼ north of Canton, South Dakota, back near the old home at Inwood. The snow was pushed back along the road in places so high that it was like driving in an open tunnel. It was thawing, and the mud on the two miles after we left the hiway to reach our new home was deep and slippery so it was late when we arrived and could get the stoves up for warmth and some beds fixed. It was the most uncomfortable move we ever made. The yard fences were down and live stock could wander at will, so fences must be fixed first. There was mud and slush everywhere but we finally created some order.

We made some arrangements for Kent to board with an old friend in Canton to continue his Sophomore year in H. School. Rodney was in fourth grade and rode Comet to country school two miles away on Hiway 77. Ruth was 6 in March so did not start to school until September. I do not remember these three years in Lincoln County as very happy ones. We were able to rent 80 A. more land from Mr. Grogan, a mile east of where we lived. Ray still farmed with horses and Kent learned to handle them pretty well. We had three new colts that summer.

We determined to get along without any more Government aid and as everything we had was mortgaged for feed and seed loans it wasn't easy, but gradually our finances improved.[3] Then sickness and doctor bills plagued us. I became pregnant again in April and spent the most of May and June under a doctor's care. By July I was able to do my work again, then one day during harvest I was suddenly stricken with convulsions and rushed to the Sioux Valley Hospital in Sioux Falls. The doctor called it eclampsia and I lost the baby.[4] Dr. Wendt may not have been the best Doctor in the world but his philosophy of life was certainly unusual. He was a great humanitarian. He taught a flourishing Sunday School men's class in the Methodist church and conducted a community orchestra of just anyone who wanted to play in it. Also a Sunday School orchestra in the church. His orchestra was

outstanding and they gave periodic concerts. All this he did
free of charge. He never sent his patients a bill. When we
finally got around to pay him for his services we remarked
about it and thanked him for it. He said, "People pay me
when they can, I've never lost anything by it, in fact, I think
I've gained."

We did not have a telephone. In November our nearest
neighbor, Mr. Cleveland, called Ray to their telephone for a
message that his father Burgess Gist had suddenly passed
away. Ray went via bus to the funeral at Wheatland, Missouri.

Our crops were good that year. We all worked at picking
the corn by hand and how grateful we were for it. It looked
like yellow gold to us who had endured so many years of crop
failure and drouth. We were not able to pay anything on our
Gov't debts, but at least we had feed for livestock, and had
raised a garden and canned vegetables and fruit for food for
ourselves. We had a nice cave near the house for storage. I
saw my first kerosene refrigerator that year.[5]

1 9 3 8

Ruth started to the country school in September 1937 with
Rodney. She was not a "pony girl," and did not enjoy riding. We decided to send Kent to Worthing to High School as it
was closer and he could drive our car from home and take
Rodney and Ruth on the way. We only had one car so that
created problems but we could barely afford to keep one car
going much less finance two.

In January Kent got an ear infection and had to have a
mastoid operation in Sioux Valley hospital in Sioux Falls. A
specialist, Dr. Nillsen, performed the surgery and we were
surely grateful for his skill and kindness as we did not have

the money at that time to pay him, so more doctor bills. His [Kent's] classmates gave him a silver agate ring while he was in hospital instead of flowers. He recovered in fine shape and finished his junior H. S. year that spring.

Ruth won a superior rating in the local Declamatory contest and got to enter the district contest. I made her a brown wool circular skirt to wear, out of an old pair of men's pants and bought a yellow sweater for the occasion. Rodney was in the contest, too, and we practiced much on "Pa Soaks his Feet." [*As an adult, Ruth had no idea what she performed for the contest but remembered very well the yellow sweater, as getting a "store-bought" article of clothing was a special event for the Gists.*]

In the summer of 1937 Mother returned from California and that fall had a complete nervous breakdown. She was living in an apartment in Inwood and would not leave there to be away from her doctor, so I spent all fall alternating with Ethel between her apartment 20 miles away and home, trying to care for her and keep our children in school. Christmas eve of 1937 we spent all day in [a] Sioux Falls clinic giving her a complete examination but the doctors found nothing seriously wrong, except nerves. Finally we decided she would have to come live with us so we fixed up our downstairs bed room and brought her home with us. Gradually she improved and spent the most of the next 14 years with us.[6]

Mont and Rena and family visited us during threshing time. They really enjoyed the activities of the threshing crew and the huge amounts of food and meals we prepared and served. There were 10 of us Gists besides the crew of 15 or 20 men. They had a tent along for camping so set it up in the yard for the boys to sleep in.

Rodney was getting too big for his little pony so decided to trade her to Art Olson who had a family of little boys, for a brown Swiss heifer calf. Thus starting a business venture for himself.

1 9 3 9

During 1938–1939 we attended the Congregational church and Sunday School in Worthing as the children's friends were all there. Kent graduated from High School that spring being second for scholarship in his class. We were very proud of his achievements, and character and wide circle of friends. He was President of his class and much involved in all the High School activities. We could not buy him many clothes but did manage a new suit which came too late for him to crown the queen. His kingly robe consisted of his Sunday pants and a maroon colored sweater. I think I felt worse about it than he did. His Aunt Opal sent him a gift of $3.00 which he spent for a cherished dream of a pair of white shoes. He kept them white. We gave him a brood sow for a gradua-tion gift. She had 6 pigs and promptly trampled and ate 4 of them. He carefully nurtured the other two in the house until they died then sold his sow and bought some clothes which he needed. He was anxious to get a job but was not 17 until Au-gust after he graduated and we thought too young to be through school, but we could see no way then to help him go to college. He got a job pitching bundles to a threshing ma-chine that summer and Ray worried all the time because he thought Kent too young for that kind of work.

After harvest we got a neighbor to do our chores and the family took a little trip to Illinois to visit Monts. This was a thrill for all of us as it had been seven years since we could take a vacation. We drove to Eula's at Griswold, Iowa, the first day then on to Beardstown. Mont and Rena had made big plans for our entertainment and we had a wonderful time. We visited Springfield, Illinois, and all of the Lincoln shrines and spent a day in New Salem park, also a day in Petersburg with Uncle Marion Torrey. Uncle Marion had a grape arbor and we sampled his exclusive brand of wine.[7]

The Clark farm where we lived was sold in 1939 which meant that we would have to move. Not having found a place

by October we made a trip to Madison to look at a place that
Uncle Fred McCracken told us about. We decided to rent it,
and prepared to move by March 1, 1940. Kent was not in
school so he and Ray moved several things that fall with the
car and trailer. Rodney went along when not in school.

Mother did not want to leave Iowa so [she] moved back
to Inwood, spending part time at Ethel's and part in an apartment at Guy Smith's.[8]

1 9 4 0

We moved to our new home two miles south of Madison
one of the last days in February. Ray had gone with a
trailer load and I was busy washing clothes when the Mc-
Cracken boys drove up in 2 big trucks to move us. We were
not ready to move and I was flabbergasted, with Ray gone.
But when those big six-footers come to move something, they
move it. They got everything loaded in good shape, the wet
clothes in the wash tub. We swept and scrubbed the floors and
took off, and found a very surprised husband.

This was the most beautiful house and location that we
have ever lived in. It was situated on a hill, and we could look
out of the north windows and see the city of Madison. The
house was a large square 2 story home with oak woodwork
and floors finished with light varnish. There was a convenient
kitchen, a dining room, a large long living room extending
across the front of the house, and 4 nice bedrooms upstairs
with clothes closets. It was furnace heated and seemed wonderful to us, moving from the small house in Lincoln County.
We even had a telephone! Our furniture nearly got lost in this
big house as all we had for the living room was a piano, roll
top desk and a library table. We soon got linoleum carpets for
the floors which helped a lot.

Rodney and Ruth started to school in the campus training school.[9] Rodney in 8th grade and Ruth 3rd. The transportation problem was solved here as a bus picked them up. We started to attend the Methodist Church and it wasn't long before Rev. Stromberg called us and we were established in Sunday School and church groups.

We brought our old Lyman County feed and seed mortgages along with us, and also $200 [of] doctor bills. Ray farmed with horses, Kent helping except part-time he worked for neighbors for wages.

Early in the spring, Ethel called me that mother was ill and that I should come down and see what to do with her. We made arrangements for her to come to South Dakota to live and brought her home with us. She was then receiving $20 per month old age assistance from Iowa and they agreed for her to live in South Dakota. We brought her own bed room furniture and gave her a large pleasant room for her own.

We bought a new oil brooder stove and raised more chickens that summer.

Rodney and Cricket, his dog, were going after cows one evening and found a swarm of bees settled on a fence post. He decided he should go into the bee business so he and Grandma made a bee hive out of a nail keg. They swabbed it out inside with sweetened water, hoping to attract the bees, and he hitched his goat to the sled and hauled it as close as he dared to the bees. They were still there, and he waited anxiously but the next day they flew away, utterly ignoring his efforts and dreams.

Ray had bought the kid at an auction sale that spring for a dime and Rodney made a great pet of it. It was cute, about like a jack rabbit when we first got it, but wasn't a very cute goat and a mighty active one. Rodney drove it in a pet parade in Madison that fall. They had a baby coyote that summer, too, which they kept in the basement. It seemed every time I removed a big tray of eggs from the incubator that it would nip my legs. One Sunday Edgar Wattenbargers from Spencer, South Dakota, came to visit us and Carroll was so enthused

over the coyote that they sold it to him for fifty cents. Was I
happy! And Edna left shaking her head in frustration.

When our home burned in 1926 near Presho we lost our
radio and had not been able to acquire another until this fall
of 1940 just before [the] election. It was a great thrill for all
of us, especially Ray.[10] [*Apparently Gladys is referring to the
thrill of owning a radio again, not to Franklin D. Roosevelt's
unprecedented election to a third term in office. Ruth can still
"see him hunched over listening to that radio." He seemed to
enjoy listening more than the other Gists, although Ruth re-
calls tuning in to "Jack Armstrong, All-American Boy", "The
Fred Allen Show," and "Amos 'n Andy," and Rodney remem-
bers listening to "The Lone Ranger" and WNAX's fiddler
"Happy Jack" on the Phillips battery-powered radio.*]

1 9 4 1

We bought a used Farmall tractor for $250 on an auction
sale and w[ere] finally able to begin mechanized farming.
It surely made field work easier and faster.[11]

Rodney was a freshman in High School and he and Ruth
were both soon playing in the school orchestra, studying violin under Mr. Duke. Ruth also started taking piano lessons
from Mrs. Elmer Hanson.[12] For Rodney's FFA [Future
Farmers of America] project, he planted ¼ A. of potatoes
that spring. They were a pretty good crop and he sold all of
the big ones and we used the small ones. He bought sheep
with the money to continue his projects.

Mont's family, Uncle Marion Torrey and Ray's brother
Charlie visited us during threshing time. There were 13 of us
and we all found a place to sleep under our big roof for a
week. Also much food and fun.

When Uncle Marion got home, in Petersburg, Illinois, he

sent Rodney and Ruth his daughter's violins. His daughter, Martina, who had been an accomplished violinist, had died with TB when a young woman and he wanted to keep her violins in the family. Uncle Marion was then 70 years old and thought he recognized some talent in our children.

Kent decided to enter college in Madison that fall. He stayed at home and drove the car or walked or hitchhiked the 3 miles, any way to get there. We were happy to have him go and cooperated in every way we could. Life was full, and busy with activities, one in college, one in High School and one in grade school.

The neighbors, [the] Stonebacks, had a musical family and their children and ours formed a Stoneback Gist orchestra, Emajean at piano, Orvin cornet, LaVonne trombone, Kent clarinet and Rodney & Ruth violins. An assortment of sound that sometimes harmonized. Kent and Orvin also played in the Madison City Band that summer. Besides all their activities I belonged to a Good Neighbor club and was chairman of our WSCS country circle.[13] I don't know how Ray kept us all going.

There was war in Europe, and an uneasy feeling, especially among veterans of World War I. Then on December 7, we had just come home from church and were listening to [the] radio and the shocking news flashed. Japan had bombed Pearl Harbor!

Life didn't seem much different at first, but soon the "Greetings" letters began to be delivered in our neighborhood as young men were drafted into the service, and appeals to invest in war bonds increased.[14]

Grandma Minerva Ann McCracken died in Elkton, Missouri, that fall and Mother and Uncle Fred McCracken went to the funeral via train.

1 9 4 2

L ife became ever more tense as war progressed. Gov't controls over business tightened and food rationing of sugar and meat became necessary.

Kent broke his wrist that summer while working with "Old Donk," one of the horses. We took him to a chiropractor doctor for treatment and have been sorry ever since, as it healed stiff and he did not regain full use of it. On August 12, his 20th birthday, he registered for the draft. He helped farm that summer but the call to service was ever on his mind, so he enlisted before his draft number came up and was sent to Aberdeen early in the fall to study radio and communications. Ray relived some horrible nightmares of his own infantry service in Europe in World War I, worrying about Kent's future.

The farm we were on was sold that year which meant that we would have to move again. We applied for a place north of Madison owned by John G. DeBoer and were accepted, paying $2/5$ of crops and $10 per A. for pasture and hay land.

We had an early blizzard that fall, on November 11, which covered a lot of corn in the fields. We had a few A. of poor yield that Ray was unable to get picked before we moved so we left it. The snow stayed on the ground until spring. The arthritis began to trouble Ray that fall and some days he was unable to work at all but he and Rodney managed to get some of the machinery and equipment moved during the winter months and I packed and labeled boxes. We were getting to be quite experienced movers by this time.

1 9 4 3

On one of the last days of February we officially moved to our new home. I took a ham to Merle Stoneback and she cooked it and served our crew a delicious dinner at noon then went along with me in the car to help get the house liveable. This home was 2 miles North and ½ West of Madison on hospital road. It was a smaller house and an older one, 4 rooms downstairs and 3 upstairs. It was situated in the middle of the section ½ mile from the gravel road and mail box. The children could still go to the campus school but the ½ mile walk and wait for [the] bus in cold weather was bad so Ray usually took them in [the] car in extreme weather to wait for [the] bus. We got Ruth a bicycle that summer so she could get the mail and ride over to play with Marian Schuld.

Rodney was now a Junior in High School and good help when not in school. We hired some help during harvest and corn picking. The cost of living and farm prices were gradually rising amid the Federal Government getting more involved with agriculture.

Our old Chevy car was about worn out so in July we traded it in on a 1937 Hudson Terraplane. We were a happy family to have a new (to us) car to drive. Rodney was now being allowed to drive alone to school social affairs. Kent was moved from Aberdeen to the regular army for boot training in April and was allowed a few days at home en route. The night he arrived a group of his friends met him at the bus station and brought him home for a welcome party. I remember he left on Easter Sunday via bus. The bus was crowded to standing room only and I shall never forget him standing in the crowd waving goodbye. I thought, "that's the way it will be from now on, crowded and herded like a bunch of cattle." We felt pretty low.

One afternoon that fall, Ray was standing on the street in Madison when a soldier rushed up to him, saluted, and said, "Pvt. Gist reporting, Sir!" Ray's jaw nearly dropped off—it was Kent. I saw them come home about supper time and wondered mildly who the soldier was with Ray but when he sprang from the car and started to the house in a run I recognized him with a scream and ran to meet him. It was his final furlough before going overseas and he decided to surprise us. We were a happy family for a few days. He got to try out the new car and some new girls and was king at our house. But the parting came again, this time for over 2 years.

We paid for our car and doctor bills and other debts this year but those old feed & seed loans still hung over us.

1 9 4 4

This was a good year except for war worries. Rodney graduated from High School in May with high honors. He had received the coveted State Farmer degree from FFA and won first in the State FFA oratory contest which entitled him to a trip to Chicago for National Competition. [*Rod remembered years later that his primary motivation in working so hard on his FFA speech, on black stem rust and how it spreads, was to show up his fellow FFAers, who had not elected him to a local office (which meant he could not travel to Brookings for the state annual convention). In Chicago he stayed at the Morrison Hotel, the same hotel in which he and his bride would stay on the first night of their honeymoon.*] This trip was a real thrill for him and we were all so proud of his achievement! Also among his High School trophies was a $50 war bond for winning 3rd in a Nat'l essay contest sponsored by Swift and Co.

He and Ruth were both active in 4H work. In February Rodney bought a black Angus calf for his project which we all watched grow. His name was Sambo, and Sambo soon learned to love all the petting and grooming that was bestowed upon him. It was this winter that Rodney became interested in oratory as he worked for the FFA contest, and Sambo made a splendid audience for practicing. It is easier to inspire a calf with oratory than some countenances that I have observed in church congregations.

We gave Rodney a brood sow for graduation, he to have half of the litter so he was a busy boy helping farm and care for his projects. He was 18 on October 4th so must register for [the] army draft.

Ray's health was not good. He had his teeth all extracted in August, which was supposed to help the arthritis in his system. Mother Leffler lived with us and was a semi-invalid.

Our land lord, John DeBoer, told us that we would have to move as he wanted to put his son on the farm, thinking it would keep him out of military service.

Ruth was in the seventh grade and it was time for her to have some projects, too, to learn the values of money. She was fast becoming style conscious so was allowed to choose the most of her own clothes as I've never considered myself much of a stylist. She sold Marian Gist a gallon pail of skim milk once or twice a week for ten cents a gallon, and as we kept leghorn hens we allowed her to have 15 Rhode Island Reds, she to have the brown eggs for spending money in return for doing some chores.[15] We got her a bicycle that summer so she could go to the mail box and sometimes over to Marian's or Patty's to play.

One P.M. I went up to the Red Cross room to roll bandages. We sat around long tables and visited as we worked. At our table was Mrs. Lee who had just received a message a few days before that her son was killed in action. Next to me was a lady whom I had not met before, the [wife of the] minister of the Church of God in Madison, whose son was then fighting on the front in Africa. As we chatted she said she was sponsoring a small group of war mothers who met every morning and prayed for their sons to come home and would I like to have them add my sons' names to their list. Of course I was grateful, but, I said, "I pray for mine every day too, but I

feel selfish if I just ask for them to come home. I ask God to
give them the wisdom and the courage to do whatever they
have to do, and not lose their Christian perspective on life, or
sense of values. But I'm weak enough to add P. S. Lord, you
know how bad we want them back." I don't see how God
could hear all the prayers going up at that time but apparently
He heard both hers and mine.

We rented a ½ section farm about five miles east of
where we were and prepared to move again. Even if the boys
were both gone we decided to try more land. Perhaps we
could hire help. This called for more equipment so Ray attended auction sales and bought some of the things he needed.
Rodney did the most of the fall plowing on the new farm and
helped move all they could that winter, before going to the
army. We sold enough cattle and hogs to finish paying off all
the old Gov't feed & seed loans.[16] What a relief!!

1 9 4 5

Rodney left for the army in February, a week before we
moved March 1st. After we bade him goodbye at the bus
station we went home and I went to bed and had a great big
cry. I thought that was all there was left to do and my morale
really hit bottom. Mother was ailing and in bed the most of
the time, Ray suffering with arthritis in his feet, so even walking was difficult and we had to get moved. But when I opened
my eyes, there were so many things to do that I got busy, and
life was full as usual.

I shut the door of the boys' room and stayed away from
it until Saturday when Ruth was home from school. We went
in with boxes and packed everything to move. We worked and
chatted and tried hard to forget about war.

Mother went to Inwood for two weeks and the McCrackens and neighbors helped us move. Mrs. Schuld and Mrs. Dimick cooked dinner for the crew in Schulds' home, then brought lunch over after we were unloaded and had fires going.

Rodney was sent to Texas, Camp Hood, for boot infantry training and frequent letters came which were cheerful and he seemed to be actually getting a kick out of his new life. But he was not very muscular and so young, we knew the physical training was really rough for awhile.

We had not heard from Kent for a few weeks and with all the fighting news we knew that he was in or near it or [we] would have heard. We were busy working long days to get settled, so that helped with the worry.

We milked 6 or 8 cows by hand and separated the cream with a hand-turned separator. There was no electricity on farms then except those with Delco plants so we still used kerosene lamps and lanterns. Windmills pumped livestock water and muscle lifted it for the house.[17]

One day in April I went to the mail box and there was a V mail letter from Kent. It had arrived in about a week and he gave his location as Iwo Jima where the fighting had been the worst. Somehow his location had escaped the censor. At least we knew where he was, and the worst fighting seemed to be over on that island.

Ruth did not have to change school[s] – a bus from the Campus still came for her. She was now in the 8th grade and school, music, and home work kept her busy. She also was confirmed into the church and studied classes for that. Then there was 4H club lessons and social activities.

The boys had both accumulated some calves during their years at home so we sold them and put their money into Gov't bonds for them. They both sent home a bond each month from army wages, so they would have a start when free.

This was a good place for us to live. We had all the land Ray could farm, and due to hard work, good prices and management we prospered. Gov't controls and taxes became more complex as the years went by, and more and more labor unions were making themselves heard.

There were 4 new farm families moved into the community that spring. Leonard Olsons, Ben Olsons, Joe Hexoms and us. The old timers had a big welcoming party for us at George Hansens so we were not long getting acquainted. We have always had wonderful neighbors, but these proved superior to any.

The farm was owned by two bachelor brothers and a maid sister who lived in Madison. They were fine folks to do business with and Ray could manage the farm in any way he wished. Some of the ground was low and in wet years hard to farm. The whole place was badly infested with weeds, some of them, such as creeping Jenny and sow thistles, were very obnoxious. We got the first crop in in good shape but by harvest the weeds were pretty bad in [the] grain. We hired young men for shocking and threshing.

The war ended in Europe that spring which brought relief to all whose loved ones were in that area, but for us the western war was still very real. Rodney came home for a short furlough in July and we knew when he left that he would be sent west to the war area. In due time we heard from him in Manila.

In September the news flashed via radio that Japan had surrendered. There was horror and sadness over the first atomic bomb and the suffering of the Japanese people, but what great relief that the war had finally ended. Kent was so tired of army life and anxious to get home, and he was only one among thousands of others. He was sent to Saipan to wait for shipment and during those weeks he nearly died with loneliness and inactivity but finally the ship came, and he landed on the West Coast November 30 and sent us a telegram. Release still took a couple of weeks but at least he was in his homeland. He made it home by Christmas and what a wonderful one it was! Rodney was still in [the] Philippine Islands but was safe and not too unhappy.

NOTES

1. Dale Jahr, *Lake County Pictorial History* (Madison, S.Dak.: Prairie Historical Society, 1976), 20.

2. The net cash income for farmers jumped from $2.3 billion to $9.2 billion a year from 1940 to 1945, and annual farm income per worker soared from $457 to $1,350, according to Gilbert C. Fite, *American Farmers: The New Minority* (Bloomington: Indiana Univ. Press, 1981), 87.

3. Ray earned only sixty-three dollars in "relief work" in 1937, after earning well over two hundred dollars in 1936.

4. The incidence of eclampsia, a relatively common toxemia of pregnancy that often induces convulsions or comas, dropped during the 1920s and 1930s, along with the infant mortality rate, which declined from 75 per 1000 children born in 1921 to 64 per 1000 in 1929. More recent textbooks reported that the cause of eclampsia was still unknown. See Richard and Dorothy Wertz, *Lying-In: A History of Childbirth in America* (New York: Free Press, 1977), 168, 210; Kenneth R. Niswander, *Obstetrics: Essentials of Clinical Practice* (Boston: Little, Brown, 1976), 221. As late as 1943, Gladys recorded $120 in outstanding doctor bills. The next year, however, no outstanding medical bills appeared in the account book.

5. Mechanical refrigerators using a variety of energy sources to propel the motors that ran the compressors replaced Americans' ice boxes between 1921 and 1944; by the latter year, 70 percent of American homes had mechanical refrigerators. Between 1920 and 1940 the cost of a refrigerator dropped from $600 to around $150. Oscar Edward Anderson, *Refrigeration in America: A History of a New Technology and Its Impact* (Princeton, N. J.: Princeton Univ. Press, 1953), 213–14.

6. From 1938 to 1945, Gladys's mother contributed between $18 and $120 a year to the household economy for her room and board. She apparently did not pay anything after 1945.

7. Before arriving in Springfield in the 1840s, Abraham Lincoln lived in New Salem until he became President in 1861. Sites of interest in Springfield, according to a 1947 guidebook, included the old Sangamon County Court House (where Lincoln practiced law) and Lincoln's law office, home, and tomb (where he, his wife, and three of his children were buried). Illinois Federal Writers' Project, Works Projects Administration, *Illinois: A Descriptive and Historical Guide*, rev. ed. (Chicago: A. C. McClung & Co., 1947), 382–96. The entire trip to Illinois cost the Gists $16.91.

8. Guy Smith was Rhodemia's daughter-in-law's brother; he owned an old hotel in Inwood.

9. This was the beginning of a long association of the Gist family with Madison's educational institutions. The Dakota Territorial Assembly established a state normal school in Madison in 1881 and classes began in 1883. Graduates took a twenty-two week course of teachers' instruction that was supposed to prepare them to teach in the territory's rural schools. Later, a "model school" — or "campus training school," in Gladys's words — opened, with primary, intermediate, and grammar levels. Students in the normal school practiced in the model

school, whose enrollment by the mid-twentieth century was limited to rural students. Originally called Madison State Normal School, the name of the college—which became a four-year college offering the bachelor's degree in 1945—was changed to Eastern State Normal School in 1921, to General Beadle State Teachers' College in 1947, then to Dakota State College and, still later, to Dakota State University. The high school from which Rodney and Ruth graduated was called Eastern High School, then General Beadle High School. See V. A. Lowry, *Forty Years at General Beadle, 1922–1962* (Madison, S.Dak.: Dakota State College, 1984), 2–7, 27, 38, 73, 100.

10. By 1940, 82 percent of American households had radios, according to Leo Bogart, *The Age of Television: A Study of Viewing Habits and the Impact of Television on American Life* (New York: Frederick Ungar, 1956), 10.

11. Ray paid $125 at the time of purchase and the rest two years later. Entering the world of mechanized farming was a mixed blessing, of course; the first year's expenses for the new tractor were $351.54. The International Harvester Farmall tractor, which came on the agricultural scene in 1924, was a great "boon to mechanized agriculture," according to Fite, *American Farmers,* 70. Its maneuverability and moderate size made it adaptable to a wide variety of tasks.

12. Ruth's and Rodney's involvement in music sent music and entertainment costs soaring. Whereas in 1940 the family had spent a total of $3.95 on those categories of expenses, in 1941 they spent $9.52 and in 1942 a whopping—at least compared to the Lyman County years—$29.47. In subsequent account books entertainment and music accounted for more than $50 a year, but that usually included one or two radio batteries at more than $8 apiece.

13. Called Ladies' Aid before 1939, the Women's Society for Christian Service was an organization for United Methodist Church women. In 1969 the group changed its name to United Methodist Women (UMW).

14. Late in 1940 Congress passed a peacetime draft (in response to the year-and-a-half-old war in Europe); the process proceeded slowly until after Pearl Harbor. Eventually more than 16 million Americans served in the armed forces, including 11.2 million in the Army, 4.1 million in the Navy, and 669,000 in the Marines. Some 333,000 were women. More than 64,000 South Dakotans served in the armed forces, (at least 1,180 from Lake County) and 1,338 died in combat. South Dakotans also contributed to the war effort in other ways: production of grain more than doubled; Red Cross volunteers produced more than 8 million surgical dressings; and citizens purchased Series E War Bonds at the rate of $185.75 per person. Ray and Gladys bought at least two war bonds worth $137.50. See Russell F. Weigley, *History of the United States Army* (Bloomington: Indiana Univ. Press, 1984), 430–37; Allan R. Millett and Peter Maslowski, *For the Common Defense: A Military History of the United States of America* (New York: Free Press, 1984), 408; World War II History Commission, *South Dakota in World War II* (Pierre, S.Dak., 1947), 7–8, 470–71, 480, 562.

15. Ernest and Marian Gist were apparently very distant relatives with whom Gladys and Ray became good friends. Ernest and Ray resembled one another physically and were often mistaken for brothers.

16. On March15,1945, the last of the federal loans, $446.85, were cleared from the Gists' books.

17. The Rural Electrification Administration (REA) was created in 1935, but North and South Dakota were the last two states to receive state programs. Only six rural electric cooperatives, serving less than 3,000 families, had been established in the state by 1941. Progress was slow after World War II, as electrification was held up by a long, bitter struggle among farmers, farm organizations, power companies, newspapers, organized labor, and municipal power companies. As late as 1950, 60 percent of South Dakotans had no electricity. In that year, however, twenty-one local co-ops formed the East River Electric Power Cooperative. This quickened the pace of construction, and by 1954 most of the area east of the Missouri River had electric lines. Harlan M. Severson, *Stepping Forward, Boldly: The Story of East River Electric Power Cooperative* (Madison, S.Dak.: Hunter Publishing, 1975), xi, 1–3, 12–44.

Gist Farm Machinery, 1930–1960

1930	1940	1950	1960
Wagon and hay rack	Wagon and hay rack	Wagon and rack	Wagon and flat rack
Spring wagon	Wagon and box		
	4-wheel trailer	Trailer and hoist	2 trailers and hoists
Corn lister	Corn lister		
	Corn planter	Planters (2)	4-row planter
Corn plow	Harrow	Plow	Plows and harrows
Seeder	Seeder		
	Endgate seeder		Endgate seeder
Binder	Binder	Binder	
Cream separator	Cream separator	Cream separator	
Shovel cultivator	Shovel cultivator	Cultivator	4-row cultivator
2 sets harness	3 sets harness		
Bobsled			
Hay buck			Farm hand loader
Hay rake	Hay rake	Rake	Rake
Mower	Mower	Mower	Mower
Disk	Disk	Disks (2)	J[ohn] D[eere] disk
		Corn picker	M[inneapolis] M[oline] corn picker
		Tractor	Allis tractor
			Farmall H tractor
		Elevator	Elevator
		Manure spreader	Manure spreader
		Weed sprayer	Weed sprayer
			Grain auger
			M[inneapolis] M[oline] feed grinder

Source: Gist family account books

Selected Gist Farm Accounts, 1930–1960

Item	1930	1940	1950	1960
Income				
Net income, cattle		$233.09	$2,702.31	$3,345.38
Net income, hogs	$ 88.30	765.04	1,129.26	
Net income, poultry	190.70	95.52	−9.19	80.98
Net income, eggs	89.76	73.31	1,138.89	1,305.52
Net income, cream	384.81	147.17	3.53	
Net income, crops	819.05	508.22	3,162.31	4,818.35
Operating Expenses				
Seed	17.50	40.11	552.65	163.42
Feed	20.25	149.74	686.87	655.99
Weed/insect spray				67.69
Veterinarian		14.05	118.34	2.30
Equipment repair/tools	136.52	18.10	489.05	603.14
Tractor maintenance			924.66	578.42
Labor/custom work/hauling	206.00	64.98	764.00	1,003.75
Living expenses				
Entertainment	48.50	3.95	64.61	
Medical	54.45	23.00	98.67	151.54
Household equipment	28.45	69.34	63.99	820.10
Groceries	304.30	185.77	509.15	712.17
Clothing	88.22	51.04	239.82	260.92
Fuel	29.35	63.23	140.26	230.81
Automobile maintenance	127.14	160.57	101.85	262.19
Highest amount on hand	46.71 (July 1)	19.42 (Mar. 6)	1,003.37 (Mar.)	4,224.93 (Feb.)
Lowest amount on hand	.30 (June 1)	.50 (July)	14.67 (June)	817.25 (Nov.)
Assets		2,332.00	15,363.30	20,965.00
Liabilities		800.00	400.00	00.00

Source: Gist family account books

RAY AND GLADYS ON THE PORCH
OF THEIR LAST FARM HOME.

THE HEALING EARTH, 1946–1959

The war was won, and the warriors came home. Life on the home front returned to "normal" — whatever that was, after a decade-and-a-half of depression and war. For the Gists of Madison, South Dakota, everything had changed. Early in 1945, Ray, Gladys, and Ruth had moved north of town to their last rented home. There they enjoyed their newfound freedom from debt, began saving money, and relished the long-awaited coming of indoor plumbing and electricity. An impressive array of new machinery reduced the rigors of farm work, and during the 1950s Ray sold the last of his work horses and milk cows.

The Gists' status as tenants may have been the key factor in their achievement of post-war prosperity. Since the bulk of their expenses for farmland in any given year consisted of two-fifths of their crop, rather than an amount set arbitrarily by a bank loan officer, the combination of steadily rising property values with relatively low prices for agricultural commodities affected their fiscal situation far less than it did farmers who owned their own land. Because the Gists' expenses were directly related to their gross profits, they had an advantage over many landowners caught between poor post-war markets and high mortgage payments.[1]

With their own lives now geographically and economically settled, the elder Gists also watched, and sometimes helped, their children build their own careers and families. Rod and Kent both took advantage of the GI Bill to attend college at General Beadle in Madison and the University of South Dakota in Vermillion, and Rod also put in a stint at the University of Iowa. Kent, restless after his adventures in the service, quickly decided that the academic life was not for him, and he returned to farming. Rod eventually turned away from his lifelong goal of becoming a doctor, got serious about his formerly perfunctory commitment to the church (he recalled having been religious "with his fingers crossed") and attended Garrett Seminary in Evanston, Illinois. Ruth finished high school, earned her teaching certificate, and began a long career in education—but not before she and a friend worked in New York for a time as airline reservationists.

Inevitably, the children married and formed their own families. Kent met his future wife, Edith Ingalls, a student at General Beadle and granddaughter of a man once held captive by the Sioux Indians, at a dance. Her date was a good friend of Kent's. Rod began courting Doris Leivestad of Inwood after she played organ at his Grandmother Leffler's funeral and would later successfully propose to her over Rhodemia's tombstone. Ruth met and married Madison's young state's attorney, Bob Spencer, after deciding that the East Coast held no future for her.

From the late 1940s through the late 1950s, a flurry of grandchildren appeared. The family also expanded geographically. Kent and Edith sought their fortunes in the Pacific Northwest, where Kent worked for a telephone company, managed a farm, and had his own artificial insemination firm. For many years he and Edith owned an apple orchard near Fruitland, Idaho, and ran their own tax processing business. After Rod's ordination, he and Doris began more than three decades of serving Methodist churches in nearly every corner of South Dakota and for one year in a small town in England. In 1979 Rod received a Doctor of Ministry degree from McCormick Seminary in Chicago. Bob and Ruth remained in Madison, where she finished her bachelor's degree and began more than thirty years of teaching in the public schools.

As the grandchildren grew up, they discovered the joys of the farm during their visits to Grandma and Grandpa Gist: the barn full of kittens, headless chickens staggering about the yard at butchering time, rides on Grandpa's tractor, corncribs to be climbed, and the novelty of using an outhouse. Other images survived the years between childhood and maturity: sleeping with hot water bottles in sloping, freezing upstairs bedrooms; wooden, moon-shaped knick-knack shelves; a flaw, or bubble, forming a wide-angle lens in a kitchen window, through which a child could peak at a panoramic view of the farmyard; a Thanksgiving ritual in which five kernels of orange, yellow, and white candy corn, nestled next to dinner plates, symbolized the five kernels of corn eaten by the Pilgrims on their first Thanksgiving, reminding the younger Gists of the hardships that their generation had thus far avoided.

Unfortunately, the grandchildren also retained vivid images of an increasingly ill grandfather. Caused in part, perhaps, by sleeping in cold fields and inhaling mustard gas during World War I, arthritis and emphysema plagued Ray throughout the last twenty years of his life, punctuating with irony the family's post-war prosperity and happiness. More and more farm work had to be hired, especially during harvest, and illness occasionally disabled Ray for weeks at a time. One granddaughter remembered him all too accurately as "long-suffering."

Another tarnish on these golden years came in the form of Ray's younger brother John. Once, in their distant Iowa past, he was the happy-go-lucky partner and housemate. By the 1950s he was a broken man, who apparently had been institutionalized in California. He arrived on the Gists' doorstep, nearly unannounced, and stayed for a year. Although Gladys had endured, over the course of her marriage, the presence of myriad relatives and in-laws requiring some sort of material or emotional aid, she refused to let this prodigal brother intrude permanently on the peace and privacy of their empty nest, and convinced Ray that John must return to the West Coast.

Despite Ray's declining health, he and Gladys traveled extensively during this period. Ruth recalled her mother's longing for travel; Gladys especially enjoyed meeting new people and seeing new places. She realized a long-held dream when she finally made a trip to the Black Hills, and they also journeyed to Illinois, Yellowstone National Park, and Kent's homes in various towns in Washington and Idaho. They traveled by train and bus, but mostly by car, and, according to Ruth, the trips remained "very cherished events" and "vivid memories" for Gladys until the end of her life. Unfortunately, by the early 1960s they became only happy islands in a sea of worry about Ray's worsening condition.

1 9 4 6

Kent decided that he wanted to continue his education so started to the university in Vermillion in January. It was hard for him to settle down to study, he seemed confused and unhappy and by spring came home to try farming. We gave him the Southwest quarter to manage and farm for himself and gradually he became adjusted. There is healing in the good earth and its natural beauty. A man gets time to think. It was good for us to have some youth and vitality to help with farm work and things went well that year.

Rodney was stationed in Manila and we heard from him regularly. In May he called us by telephone and we all got to talk to him. That was a great thrill, talking half way around the world. Grandma Leffler even talked to him without crying. We had notice the night before from the San Francisco operator to expect the call or we would probably all have been too excited to speak. The call was to come about 6 P.M. so we all gathered around the supper table expectantly. The call didn't come, and chores must be done so we agreed not to answer the phone until everybody could get back in the house and ready. Work all finished, and still no call. We drank coffee until about 9 P.M. the phone rang and we heard his voice.

[*Rod described the call in a letter dated May 14, 1946. He had risen at 5:30 A.M. to make the call, and had to wait some time before it went through. "It was very hard to hear Mom at first," he wrote. "I guess we were both hollering hello at the same time." Kent's voice had been "entirely unrecognizable," whereas Ray "sounded natural, but his voice didn't seem to carry very well." He could hardly hear Grandma Leffler, but "it was really grand just to hear her say 'hello.' " He thought it odd that only Ruth asked a question: "What time is it?" The call cost him $20, but it was worth it "to talk half way around the world!" He agreed with Kent: "I'll bet the party line was really busy with rubber necks."*]

June 8 was our 25th wedding anniversary and I dreamed

of a few days' trip to the Black Hills to celebrate but things did not work out so we could go. I was really disappointed. We received an invitation to Kathryn Comp's wedding in Presho June 6 so went there for a little trip but I could not enjoy it for wanting to go on.

Ruth was now 15, and Kent was home so they took care of the farm. While we were gone Ruth's music teacher, Mrs. Swan, had her piano recital. We hated to be gone for that, but Kent and his current girl friend Rosie O'Brian took good care of Ruth. They helped her into her first formal dress and Kent bought her a corsage so it was a big occasion for her.

In August we attended the biennial LTAC picnic in Inwood and visited with many old friends there for a day. They had a little special for our 25th anniversary during the afternoon program and presented us with a gift of $25. We bought a red platform rocker with the money.

In November Rodney came home from the army. How wonderful to all be together again! Rodney entered General Beadle college in Madison at the beginning of the second quarter. He wanted to become a Doctor so planned for a long siege of educating himself. He had saved his money well while in the service. He got a job as kitchen helper in East Hall to work for his board, and shared a room with Roy Jensen. Again we had one in High School and one in college and Kent at home.

1 9 4 7

Our family were all at home again this year and Grandma Leffler was still living with us the most of the time. Her health was getting worse and she required more care. Pills were as regular as food. Much of her trouble was nerves and she took too many barbituates and sleeping pills. There were many trips to the doctor and when her condition got too bad we took her to a hospital in Rock Rapids, Iowa, for treatment.

Rodney attended the summer session of college, driving the car from home, and Kent continued farming with us. Ruth started her junior year in High School in September.

We were able to finance more machinery every year now and farming became easier and more profitable.

In July, while Grandma was visiting at Inwood, we left the boys to run the farm and Ray, Ruth and I took a two weeks' trip to visit relatives in Illinois and Missouri. We went to Beardstown, Illinois, to visit Monts for a few days and when we arrived we found Charlie and Fred Gist already there so the four brothers had a good time together. We took Charles and Fred to their home in Wheatland, Missouri, when we left Illinois. We stopped in Jefferson City on the way and toured the [state] capitol.

We visited in Wheatland for a few days with relatives then went to Miller, Missouri, and took Aunt Adda Paris [*Gladys's Aunt Lucy Adeline Leffler Paris*] with us to Picher, Oklahoma, to spend a day with Dode (George) Leffler's family. Three of Uncle Dode's married children were there to greet us. John and Lelia, and Elizabeth had flown in from Topeka, Kansas, to be with us. That was a most interesting trip, as Picher is a mining town and the great piles of white chat, refuse rock, and small samples of bright colored rocks on display at the souvenir stands were all new to me.[2]

We took Aunt Adda back to her home in Miller then drove to Kansas City next day to visit nephews and relatives

there. We were happy to find Uncle Bob and Aunt Jessie Torrey at Jim Marshalls' [*James B. Marshall was the son of Ray's
sister Edna and her husband, Harry B. Marshall.*] in Kansas
City, and they were all ready to come home with us to South
Dakota. We had a pleasant two day trip with them coming
home, stopping along the way at points of interest.

When we got home a telephone call informed us that
Eula and Joel Boone [*old friends from the Lefflers' days in
Missouri*] were on their way to visit us so Ruth and I found
our vacation suddenly over and we had to hustle to entertain.

The boys cut grain for harvest while we were gone and
we told them if they got too busy they could get the neighbor
Hexom girls to cook dinners for them. It didn't take long for
them to get too busy as they went after the girls the day we
left. We got a card from them to stay as long as we liked, they
were doing fine. But the night before we got home they had
cooked themselves some supper and let the kerosene stove
smoke up the walls and ceiling of [the] kitchen. It was a beaut
of a place to cook for company.

In August Jim and Helen Marshall stopped by on their
way west for a vacation and invited us to go to Yellowstone
with them. Ray left the decision to me, but bad as I wanted to
do it, I felt we shouldn't for we had just spent our vacation
money and Grandma was with us and best not to leave her.

1 9 4 8

This was a busy happy year for all of us. Our family were all grown up, all at or near home and all busy with their activities.

Kent had bought himself his first car and was pretty busy courting when not farming. Ruth was a junior in High School that fall and in a flurry of school activities.

Rodney attended college, rooming at Herby Jensen's and working for his board in the kitchen at the girls' dormitory. He was President of the student body and involved in all of the campus activities. We were very proud and interested in all of their achievements, helping them in every way that we could.

We traded the last two of our horses, old Molly and Fronzie, to McCool for a feed grinder that spring, so our farming was completely motorized.[3]

Our poultry flock had grown into a sizeable egg income with which I ran the household expenses. The men raised around 100 hogs and were shifting from dairy to Her[e]ford cattle.

For a long time I had been dreaming of a bottled gas range for the kitchen. The old Perfection 3 burner kerosene stove without oven often smoked, and carrying fuel for the kitchen range was becoming irksome, especially in summer. In March we bought a new Tappan gas range which was the most beautiful that I could find. How happy Ruth and I were to have it to use! Grandma and Ray were a little afraid it might blow up but they just had to grin and bear it.

[*Ruth recalled that her mother "didn't hold out on something she wanted" too often, but that because Ray kept dragging his feet on buying a new stove (apparently one of the legacies of the fire back in the late 1920s was his leariness about buying a bottled-gas stove), she announced one day that she was going to town to buy one whether he wanted it or not. Later, when a minor explosion singed Ruth's eyebrows and hair, she and her mother resolved never to tell Ray.*]

There was still no electricity on farms except Delco plants and we didn't have that.[4] We used Aladdin kerosene lamps with a mantle for reading. They gave good light but were never safe from smoking and an unpleasant chore to keep the chimneys clean and lamps filled and in repair.

Rodney got infection in his leg in May and was hospitalized for about a week with that and Ruth fell while playing tennis in November and broke her arm. Grandma Leffler was a semi-invalid, in and out of bed.

Kent and Edith [Ingalls] were married June 6, 1948, in her home near Bryant, South Dakota.[5] We were happy with his choice, and happy to see him so happy. It was time for him to find fulfilment of his life in a home of his own. They had a lovely home wedding and Edith and her mother had spent many happy hours working together getting ready for it. They were married in the afternoon and by evening were headed west in their car planning to stay in Washington State and make a home. Grandma was in bed the day of the wedding so Aunt Mary McCracken [*Uncle Fred's sharp-tongued and harsh-tempered wife*] stayed with her while we all went.

Ruth and Pat Streeter won a purple ribbon and trip to the state fair in Huron in September with a 4H club demonstration [on making furniture polish].

Rodney finished all of the Science education he could get [at General Beadle] and decided to enter the U. at Iowa City, Iowa, to continue pre-med. He still had his army bonds and was eligible for G. I. education[6] help so thought he could finance it if he had a trailer to batch for room and board. We helped him finance a small one and as he had no car, Ray and his brother Charles, who was visiting us at the time, took Rodney and his trailer to Iowa City. They wouldn't allow a single man to park his trailer in the regular court so he had to park it in a private yard about 15 blocks from campus.

1 9 4 9

With both of the boys gone Ray was alone with the farming again so the job of milking 8–10 cows by hand was time consuming and irksome. Ruth and I did it sometimes in the evenings and always helped but I can't say that we enjoyed it.

That spring Emmett Yerigan, who was hauling eggs for a Brookings hatchery, stopped by to offer us [a] deal for hatching eggs, they to bring us some roosters. One evening after dark a young man delivered the roosters and the next morning one was dead. The others obviously had the chicken pox.[7] We were sure mad to have our flock of 600 hens exposed at the height of the laying season. The hatchery owner expressed regrets and vaccinated all of the hens but the egg production fell to nearly none. We finally, after threatening to take the matter up with the state poultry association, got 300 baby chicks without charge from him for settlement.

I had saved over $100 of egg money to pay for the chicks, so Ruth and I went to Sioux Falls shopping for her graduation clothes and spent it all; we really had a day and both enjoyed it a lot. Ruth graduated from [General] Beadle High School May 24, 1948, as President of her class and with high scholastic honors. She was also President of her class during her sophomore year. She was an accomplished pianist and did lots of accompanying around town for various organizations.

[*Many years later Ruth also remembered the shopping spree fondly; it was the "first time we'd ever had that much money to spend at one time." They bought a suit, high heels, and a hat, and Ruth "thought I had the world by the tail." Unfortunately, when she arrived for the graduation ceremonies, she discovered that another girl had a new suit exactly like hers!*]

We still did not have electricity on the farm, so bought our first mechanical refrigerator (bottle gas) from Leonard Brown who was converting to electric. I thought it a wonderful convenience. Many people by this time had either gas or kerosene operated refrigerators.

We did not yet own a combine, so hired Norm Stoneback to combine 50 A. of oats at $3.50 per A. and cut 60 A. with the binder, shocked and threshed it.

Ray was not very well that fall and when the neighbors got thru picking their corn they had a "picking bee" for us and finished what we had left to harvest. In November we took the crew and their wives to Thomsha's diner for a turkey dinner, then back to the farm for a party and late refreshments.

Weed spraying with chemicals was becoming popular so we bought ⅓ interest in a new sprayer with Elmer Burns and Joe Hexom that summer and it proved to be a very good investment.[8]

About June 1 we went to Iowa City and brought Rodney's trailer home. He didn't have much chance of studying medicine in Iowa City so decided to go to Vermillion U. [*University of South Dakota*] that fall and get all the pre med he could there. In September we parked his trailer in the most convenient place that he could find near the campus and he entered there.[9]

Ruth entered [General] Beadle College in Madison so now we had two in college. Ruth roomed in the girls' dormitory and worked in the dining room for her board. They both worked for a lot of their expenses and we helped them in every way that we could.

On April 13, 1949, our first grandchild was born. Sara Beth Gist was born near Arlington, Washington, and it was a year before we got to see her.[10]

1 9 5 0

This was a good year. Our interests spread with our children and we all grew. Rodney took examinations in Vermillion to enter medical training and after sweating that out found he was accepted. But for over a year we could see that he was not quite happy with that calling, that he was praying and struggling with the decision of changing to the ministry. There are times when it is best for parents to just stand by and pray for them, but to withhold advice unless asked for it. Either choice was fine with us. He came home one week end that winter and announced that he had given up his place in medical school and was going to train for ministry in the Methodist Conference. We were quite happy with his decision.

Kent and Edith came home around April 1 and Kent attended the Curtis Candy artificial insemination[11] school in Chicago for two weeks, leaving Edith and the baby to visit us and the Ingalls. Sara was a darling baby but she was afraid of everybody so we hardly dared to touch her. She soon made up with Grandpa tho. [*Kent later recalled that when Sara finally crawled into her grandpa's lap, Ray "took the rest of the day off" and carried his first grandchild on a tour around the farm.*] When Kent returned from school they went west again, this time to Meridian, Idaho.

We went to Vermillion in June to see Rodney receive his B.S. degree. He sold his trailer there and came home to help farm for the summer.

Ruth also spent the summer at home.

Ray bought another H tractor that spring on a sale and at harvest time he bought a new Case combine which he had been wanting for a long time. No more grain shocking or bundle hauling for a threshing machine. It certainly eliminated a lot of hard work.

During harvest, Mont and Rena came to visit us and when harvest was finished the men came in one day and Mont said, "Ray and I have decided we can take a little trip now. Gladys, is there any place that you would like to go?"

Immediately I answered, "Yes, to the Black Hills!"

The next day we were off! I could hardly believe it, a long cherished dream come true. We toured the Badlands. I hadn't imagined them looking like that and found them the most fascinating terrain that I have ever seen. The formations and colors are beautiful.[12] We spent the night in Wall, entertained by the famous Wall Drug cowboy display,[13] then on to Rapid City for breakfast. We visited the [Mount Rushmore] National Monument and scenic places and parks, and spent the next night in a Hill City tourist cabin. The next morning we drove a little more for scenery, visited a fish hatchery[14] and came home a different road thru Phillip and Pierre, so saw a lot of South Dakota. I even enjoyed the miles of prairie which Mont called so much of nothing. It was a wonderful vacation for me.

In September Rodney bought an old Plymouth car and drove it to Chicago to enter the Seminary at Garrett.[15]

Ruth went back to Beadle in Madison for her second year of teacher training.

We hired Blaine Johnson to run the corn picker for corn harvest.

It was a good crop, so we decided to spend it for another car. The old Terraplane had served our family well. It needed repairs, which were hard to find and one can always think of dozens of reasons for a new car. We bought a 1950 nearly new dark green Packard for $2050 and the Terraplane. It was the best car that we have ever owned and a pleasure to drive. We used it for ten years with little trouble. Our family all drove and enjoyed it.

We attended the State Fair in Huron that fall which was a big thrill for me. It had been a long time since we had attended a State Fair.[16] We went to most of the college affairs put on for the public and enjoyed hearing about all their activities.

We quit milking cows as the cattle were mostly Hereford and not having enough pasture we sent the most of them to be pastured near Strandsburg, South Dakota.

1 9 5 1

We now had a nice herd of cattle and Ray kept a lot of hogs. Ray sold over $5500 of hogs in 1951, also $2100 of eggs from a big flock of leghorn hens.

The farms all around us were being electrified and our land lord, Ed Sponholtz, made arrangements to have ours wired. In January the power was released to our farm.[17] What a wonderful thing to have, and it opened up a whole new era of conveniences. At first the freedom from kerosene lamps and old flat irons that had to be heated on the kitchen range was most appreciated. I had a gasoline iron which was a little better than flat irons but it never held enough gas for all the shirts. I ironed without a refill and a lot of pumping air into it. We used it in hot weather tho. Gradually we acquired small appliances, toaster, mixer, fans, etc.

We bought a new gas brooder stove which was also a great convenience from regulating a kerosene brooder. The gas was automatic.

Mother was 80 years old February 13, and getting pretty frail. She had to have a doctor and needed professional care so often that at her request in the fall of 1950 we made arrangements to put her in a Good Samaritan home for the aged near LaVerne, Minnesota. In August of 1951 she was transferred to the hospital in Rock Rapids, Iowa. We visited her often and cooperated with her care as much as possible.

While we were harvesting grain on the south quarter August 11, 1951, I was called to the hospital. We rushed to her bedside and sat with her all night and the next day. After a blood transfusion she seemed better so Ethel and I went to Inwood to get some rest. The next morning we called again and when we got there, she was gone. I was sorry we had not stayed with her. We had the funeral in the Inwood Methodist church and buried her in the cemetery one mile east of Inwood beside my father. Ruth was working in Wall, South Dakota, and came home, and Rodney from Chicago and many other relatives and friends. [*Actually, Ruth worked in a restaurant-motel-gas station at a place called Seven-Mile Corner, between Kadoka and Wall near the Badlands. She lived with two other girls in one room and with them spent her free time touring the Badlands and attending rodeos and "wild west dances."*]

September 1, Ruth started her teaching career in Huron, Rodney still in seminary.

In September after we were alone again we hired Herby Jensen to do the plowing and look after our livestock, and we took a three week trip to visit Kents, then on to Arlington, Washington, to visit [Gladys's brother] Ira and Myrtle. I had never been out of the midwest, most all of my travelling had been done via books or visitor's descriptions. We had an AAA [American Automobile Association] travel guide which we studied every night and I rode with it open to recognize and read the descriptive and historical values of interesting places along the way. Deadwood [South Dakota] is a most intriguing city built on the side of a mountain. Its streets seem to run any convenient way and Main Street is made of cobblestones. Most everybody had several flights of steps to go down to reach Main Street if they walked.[18]

Early morning was the best time to travel as the scenes were so fresh, and wild animals were more likely to be browsing around. I shall never forget my first view of the Rockies as we approached the Big Horns from Buffalo, Wyoming. Their majestic heights were snow capped and they were shrouded in a purple mist. It gave me a feeling of awe and reverence. How would we ever get over them?

It was late in the season when we registered at the gate of Yellowstone [National Park] and the most of the lodges were closed but they were not of much interest to us anyway. We drove in scenic wonderland all day. The most unforgettable sights were artist and inspiration points, the mud volcanoes, water falls and hot springs. We waited an hour for Old Faithful to erupt and it was beautiful in the sunlight. I bought a necklace and ear ring souvenirs at the lodge. We left Yellow-

stone by the south gate and drove to Jackson, Wyoming, with
the beautiful Tetons to the west of us. There was always something fascinating and interesting to see, even in the deserts.

We spent a wonderful week visiting and sight seeing with
Kents around Jerome, Idaho. Sara had grown so much and
could talk now.

Then northwest to Washington. We crossed the Columbia
River by ferry, visited the Fergusons in Yakima, saw hops
growing and big grain fields. When we crossed over the top of
the Cascades we met an army convoy and drove awhile with
them on our left, the high side, and on our right the edge of
the road with a sheer drop down into a white cloud and
space. It was like meeting Gabriel's chariots in the sky.

Ira and Myrtle took us to Everett then via ferry across
Puget Sound to a Peninsula then drove to Bremerton to see
the big ships and navy yards.[19] From there a larger ferry to
Seattle which took about an hour. We toured Seattle.

From Iras we went via Wenatchee Valley and Coulee Dam
back to Kent's.[20] Then home and our straight South Dakota
roads really looked good.

1 9 5 2

For the first time, we started the year free of debts. What a
comfortable sense of well being! There was no one home
but just us to use the car so it was always available. We
missed the children's music and activities.

On February 15 we received a telephone call from Kent
that Melissa Rae was born.[21] A happy little Valentine and us
too far away to even see her!

Ruth came home for summer vacation then back to Huron to teach in September. Rodney also came home but was
anxious to be about his work in the ministry, so found work
in a little church in Wisconsin for the summer. He wrote inter-

esting experiences home. In September he returned to Garrett to finish Seminary and worked in a church in the stock yard district of Chicago to help earn his expenses and further his education.

We bought a new wool rug for the living room and a vacuum cleaner. I love the luxury of carpeted floors.[22]

During the first of November Ray got an ulcer in his eye, caused by an injury while picking corn. He was hospitalized with it for about a week and finally went to a specialist in Sioux Falls to have it burned off. While he was confined to the house Kent's family drove in one evening from Idaho. Were we glad to see them!

The children were all home for Thanksgiving but there came a big blizzard snow storm the day before which caused a lot of frustration. It was cozy inside, best not to look out. Rodney got stuck in Blue Earth, Minnesota, on the way home and was delayed overnight so only got to be here about 24 hours. Kent drove on ice one whole day on their way back to Jerome, Idaho. Everybody gone and we were alone again. Must let them be free and enjoy our own life.

1 9 5 3

Rodney and Ruth both came home for Easter vacation. It was too short.

When school was out in Huron Ruth decided she wanted to try something besides teaching, so applied and was accepted for employment by the Northwest Airlines in Minneapolis. After a short training course she was assigned to work as a reservationist in New York City beginning in July.

Rodney was in the last weeks of his seminary education. We helped him finance them.[23] By this time he had, along with his academic education, learned to handle money wisely.

He was ready to get married and eager to start his career.
Leaving Herby Jensen to run the farm in June we took Ruth,
Ethel and Raymond along and drove to Chicago to see him
graduate and attend his wedding. Immediately after the graduation exercises he and Doris [Leivestad] were married in the
little chapel on the Garrett Campus.[24] It was a lovely wedding
with only our immediate families and a very few close relatives as guests. Ruth and Muriel [Leivestad] were bridesmaids
and Arthur Erickson and another college friend of Rodney's
as his attendants. Rodney's best friend Ronald Hartung performed the ceremony. After the ceremony we were taken to
the church where Rodney was working and they gave them a
heart warming reception.

It was an interesting trip to Chicago as I had never been
there before. On the way we stayed overnight in a motel near
Madison, Wisconsin. While walking around the motel I saw a
little boy about five years old tip over on his tricycle. He
didn't cry but got up emanating sullen defiance to everybody
and everything. He was the dirtiest child I ever saw. I shall
never forget him and have often wondered about his home,
and what kind of man he grew up to be.

We stayed in Chicago 3 days and saw lots of interesting
sights. The things that impressed me most w[ere] the great
expanse of the lake [Michigan], the boats, and the landscaped
flower gardens on the campus at Garrett and the little chapel.
The chapel was an inspiration.[25]

We came home by Mont's and visited there for three
days, then to Inwood with Ethel and Raymond, then home.
My peonies which were in bud when we left were about gone.

Ruth flew from Sioux Falls to New York City in July.
With parental love and trepidation we saw her plane take off.
She had to try her wings alone. Rodney had some summer
school to finish in Chicago and Kent in Idaho so we were
indeed alone in South Dakota now. In September Rod and
Doris came back to South Dakota to begin their first ministry
in Viborg, South Dakota. They were busy and happy.

When the weather got cool we bought a new oil burning

heating stove for the living room. Up to this time we had burned coal in a heater. How glad I was to be rid of soot and ashes and fuel carrying! It didn't heat the big house in cold weather. We still had to have the coal stove in the dining room, but at least I had it off of my wool rug.

Ruth flew home from New York City for Christmas and decided that she did not want to go back and we were glad of it. She found a new boy friend, Bob [Spencer],[26] over the holidays and as there seemed no opening to teach at that time she entered G[eneral] B[eadle] College again to work for her degree.

[*After being laid off by Northwest Airlines, Ruth was offered a job with Eastern Airlines in Florida, but she turned it down and returned to finish her education in South Dakota.*]

1 9 5 4

Ray traded the old Farmall tractor in on a newer model Allis Chalmers and bought a loader. Both [were] mighty convenient.

Ruth went to college all summer to finish her junior year. She won a KSI scholarship which helped with the financing. [*The scholarship from Kappa Sigma Iota, an honor society, helped with Ruth's educational expenses, but she also worked for her mother's cousin, Wally Leffler, for her room and board in Madison.*]

During her vacation in August she went with us and we made a trip to Kent's in New Plymouth, Idaho. We went a southern route this time, thru Estes and Rocky Mountain Park, Colorado, to Salt Lake City spending an afternoon in the famous Mormon square.[27] I love to ride in the mountains, each new scene is a thrill.

It was wonderful to be with Kent's family again, and

interesting to learn about his work for artificial insemination of dairy cattle. They used egg yolk with the semen and I watched Kent pick up egg yolks with his fingers to separate it from the egg white. After all the eggs I had cooked in my life I was amazed that it could be done.

They took us on a trout fishing trip for two days way up in the mountains. We cooked steak and corn on the cob over a camp fire and was it good! I stayed in camp with Sara and Melissa while the others walked up the mountain stream to fish. We decided to decorate a little Christmas tree with aluminum foil strips and anything we could find. There was a purse for Mother, a scarf for Ruth, a tool for Daddy but we couldn't find anything for Grandpa. The next thing I knew there was an array of precious angle worms dangling from the tree for Grandpa that he and Kent had dug.

We came home via the shortest route thru Rawlins, Wyoming, and Presho but it poured rain so we dared not get off the hiway to visit any old friends there so we came on home arriving about noon. Ruth phoned Bob at once but he was out of town. Sad girl!

Dalton Williams and Herby Jensen picked our corn.

During this year, in February I think, one of the jewelry stores in Madison was sold out at auction by the sheriff and we bought a service of silver for 8 in a chest. It is Gorham and I was real thrilled to have nice silver. We also got 3 pieces of Ruth's sterling pattern.

We spent a lot of time and some money during these years working on family genealogy. Miss Jean Dorsey of Urbana, Illinois, helped us and it was very interesting research.[28]

In June, Aunt Jessie Torrey from Los Angeles, California, visited us. She was 77 years [old] and a lively charming guest. Uncle Bob [had] died January 2, 1948.

December 20, 1954, another granddaughter was born to Rodney and Doris at Viborg, S.D.[29] Rodney was almost beside himself with excitement and joy. We drove down the next day to see her—something we hadn't been able to do with Kent's children. Now we could have the pleasure of loving and watching her grow.

1 9 5 5

We were able to afford several new conveniences this year. When Aunt Jessie Torrey got home from visiting us, she wanted to do something nice for us, so sent us a check to buy a new T. V. set. The most of our neighbors had one. We enjoyed it very much when alone, especially evenings, but it always irked me to go call on a neighbor and have to listen to their T. V. all evening, unless for a special program. I went to visit and never did like to compete with a T. V. or radio. The novelty soon wore off with most people tho.[30]

The greatest convenience I ever had was a water system installed in the kitchen in August.[31] Turn a faucet and get hot or cold water running into a big double sink. It was piped out into the back yard for the first year but we could walk around a mud hole that drained away from the house. Before that I pumped water by hand from a cistern, carried it into the house then out after it was used. Heated laundry water in a big copper boiler on the kitchen range. I did have an electric motor on my Maytag washing machine. The advent of electricity certainly lifted the drudgery from farming.

Ray bought a new grain elevator, flat hay rack, loading auger and in the fall a new two row corn picker. All this for us without assuming a heavy load of debt.

Ruth graduated "Magna cum laude" with a B[achelor of] S[cience] degree in June and was hired to teach in the campus grade school in September. Kents came home and were here for her graduation. We had a family dinner for her and Edith's sister Dorothy in our home after the morning exercises.

That summer Marion and Evalyn Gist from Yucaipa, California, came to visit us and Mont and Rena came while they were here so the brothers and all of us had a good time visiting for a few days.

December 26 Ruth and Bob Spencer were married in a small private ceremony. Rodney and Doris had been transferred to First Methodist Church in Sioux Falls as assistant

pastor so just the immediate family went there and Rodney
performed the ceremony in his church. It was a very cold day.
Doris fixed a lovely wedding dinner for all of us and they
were off for a short honeymoon then back to establish their
first home in a little apartment in Madison.

1 9 5 6

Our family was growing fast. A new son-in-law in December
and two new grand children in 1956. About noon on May
23 Kent phoned us that they had a son! We could have heard
him without the phone if we had been listening. John Watson
was the first grandson.[32] Now Grandpa J. R. would have
someone to carry on his name of Gist.

On October 19, Rodney phoned that they had another
daughter in Sioux Falls. We rushed down to see her and she
was a darling little black haired baby Linda Carol.[33] We had
to love Kent's children from far away, but Rodney's we could
enjoy. We could have them with us sometimes when Rodney
and Doris were away on trips or vacation, besides the family
calls.

In November after the corn was picked, we got George
and Nora Hansen to stay in our home and do chores and we
took a trip to Ripon, Wisconsin, to visit Ray's sister Opal. We
had never been in her home nor heard much from her during
the last 30 years. She was married the second time now and
had no children. We stayed two days and they entertained us
royally showing us many interesting things. We visited the
little house in Ripon where the Republican party was
formed,[34] had dinner in Oshkosh and saw the overall factory.[35] Opal cooked us a lobster dinner. I had never eaten lobster and thought it delicious but Ray was not enthused. Opal's
husband Ernie took time from work and showed us the lakes

at Winneconne and beautiful country drives. It seemed to me
there is a tavern on every corner clear across Wisconsin.

From there we went to Beardstown, Illinois, and spent a
week with Monts. We always have such a good time with them
and their families. Then on again thru the timbered country
so different from our prairie, to Wheatland, Missouri, to
spend Thanksgiving day with Charles's family in Oral's home.
All of Charles's children and grandchildren were there. He
really has a nice family and they treated us as honored guests.
Later we visited Fred's families in Bill's and Lola's homes and
the bonds of family ties were drawn a little closer. The
weather was cold and raw. I nearly froze every time I got
outside but it was a jolly time inside. We spent overnight and
a day with my Dad's sister Aunt Adda Paris at Miller, Missouri, then to Kansas City for a stop over with the Marshalls
and Aunt Corda Moore and McCracken relatives in Liberty. It
was a happy two weeks of visiting and eating.

The place we sold our eggs, Wenks Produce in Madison,
gave a trading point system, instead of trading stamps which
were becoming so popular. Having many eggs to sell we soon
had a lot of points so got a Royal typewriter with them. I told
the kids I packed and sold nineteen thousand dozen clean eggs
to win that prize. I can use this pen as fast as that but I enjoy
trying.

It was pretty nice to have Bob in the family now. He did
our income tax report for us which was always a headache.
He did it to our advantage, too, as he saved us $100. We had
been just too generous with our Uncle Sam.

1 9 5 7

With the machinery we had acquired over the last few years, we were able to do the most of our 320 A. farming alone now hiring only a few days of help, usually machine hire such as hay baling, trucking, etc. These were happy years, working together.

Kents came home for a few days in May and our family was together again. The children all growing so fast, and we hardly got acquainted before they were gone.

We were eating lunch one day in August during the oats combining season when the phone rang and it was John's ex-wife Mathilde in California telling us that John was sick and needed help. We couldn't seem to get much particulars but had John's son Donald's address so Ray wrote to him, and before we had time to get an answer Mathilde phoned again, urgently, so Ray sent Donald a check for $50.00 and wrote him some fatherly advice on how to use it. A few days later a letter came saying they were sending John to us with some of Mathilde's car racing relatives who were going to Minneapolis to enter some races. Donald gave them the money to get there and bring John here. August 23 he arrived on our door step with a carton of rummage clothing. We were never so shocked and astonished in our lives! We hadn't seen or heard much from him for 30 years, and here he was, a broken old man, destitute and mind half gone from ravages of liquor, family trouble and loneliness.

My mind flew back across the years to the time when we were all young and farming together near Inwood, Iowa. John was a handsome, gay fellow with curly, wavy hair which the girls all adored, but he hated it and kept it cut short. He had a habit of singing all the popular songs and funny little dittys [sic] as he went about his work, and now and then dancing a jig from pure joy of living. One morning he sang me a song about a deacon getting drunk at the altar of holy communion. He thought it very funny, but it did not strike me in that way.

I remembered going for a walk in the clean air, trying to get my sense of values straight. John did not mean to be sacreligious. He hadn't the slightest idea of the meaning or strength one could derive from holy ritual.

When he moved into our spare bedroom I knew it was for the rest of my life unless we did something about it. We fed, clothed, tobaccoed and kept him clean for a year. He was eager to please and capable of helping Ray when he worked with him but could not run machinery or do anything alone. He seemed to want to help me with everything I did, like a subnormal child. We spent a year of heartache and worry trying to help him and decide what to do with him. We had to decide within a year before he lost his citizenship [residency] in California. I never spent so many sleepless nights or prayed so hard over anything in my life. He was younger than either of us and Ray's health [was] failing. Should we accept the responsibility or send him back?

[After a] year we sent him back to Santa Rita Rehabilitation Center near Berkeley, California, where he had been the most of the 15 years before he came here. We never did find out why he was away from there.

1 9 5 8

We still kept a flock of around 500 laying hens and sold about $2000 eggs that year which paid the most of our living expenses.

We transferred our Postal Saving account to the Building and Loan as it drew 4% interest there and only 2% in Postal Savings.[36]

I've always enjoyed gardening and by this time it contained more flowers than vegetables. I tried about every kind of flower that would grow here and some that didn't. We didn't buy many vegetables as there was always plenty in the cellar. This year we bought a new electric refrigerator with freezing compartment across the top. We also kept a rented freezer in [the] Madison locker plant. [*The Gists rented a meat storage locker, usually for around $15 to $20 a year, from 1948 to 1963.*]

On August 16 we sent John via bus back to Berkeley, California. We never heard from any of them again until 1965, he wrote us that he was well and living in a nice place evidently in a mission in Sonoma, California.

Monts visited us in October and we drove to Pierre to see the Oahe dam which was under construction and again visited the capital to note any changes.[37]

We decided to spend Christmas with Kent's family so hired a young couple, Bob Francis and wife, to stay on the farm and we went via bus to Omaha then on the train to Ontario, Oregon, where Kent met us. It was our first train travel in years and we enjoyed it. I felt real elegant eating in a diner. We explored the dome car and other [changes in] train facilities that had taken place in the last forty years.

It was a Happy Christmas. We went as a family to Christmas eve communion service at the church. Edith and Kent had open house for us one Sunday and we met many of their friends, and were entertained by some of them in their homes while there. We visited a big sugar factory and many places of interest. The three weeks went by all too fast.

When we came home, Rodney and Doris met us in Omaha to save us the night wait and bus ride home. It was good to be back and we had so many pleasant memories to re-live through the long South Dakota winter.

1 9 5 9

This was an eventful year. Kirby Austin Spencer was born June 5th in Madison, and we were so happy to have another grandson arrived safely.[38] From the first, Grandpa fussed over him like a mother hen. As soon as Kirby could walk they made a great pair, exploring the farm, taking care of the animals and machinery. The summer he was three they found a nest of baby rabbits on the lawn and watched the gulls flying over the tractors in the fields. A blackbird made a nest in the vine on the front porch and we set the step ladder so he could perch on top and watch the eggs and babies hatch while the parent birds sputtered and scolded but he did not harm them. We had a hired man, Oscar, the summer Kirby was four and taking lunch to the field was a big thrill, Grandpa with a thermos of coffee and Kirby a bottle of pop which he learned to carefully save until they got there if he wanted to drink with the men. At first he was scared to death of the tractors and screamed every time the motor started. Besides, the thing usually took Grandpa away. But he learned to love to ride on Grandpa's lap around the yards. I asked him later if he could remember those things and he said the thing he remembered most was when they pulled Leonard Olson's tractor out of a mud hole.

Our big farm house had a pantry adjoining the kitchen which was used to store food, medicines, utensils and everything else that we did not know what to do with. We had the cream separator installed in a corner when we milked cows by hand, carried the milk to the house in pails, ran it thru the hand turned separator, then carried the skim milk back to the barns for the calves and pigs. Washing the separator and pails was an every morning chore. The separator had 36 steel discs that fitted into a heavy bowl and the centrifugal force thru these separated the cream and milk. We had quit milking any cows by 1959 and bought our milk now so had disposed of all the milking equipment.

Since having electricity I dreamed of having the pantry remodeled and a bath room installed. Our land lord said he would put in a septic tank and do that for us so I went to work on the room. I never knew an old fashioned pantry could hold so much cluttery stuff but I finally got it empty and before cold weather we had all the conveniences of city life.[39]

Every summer we had company from away. This year was Uncle [Le]Roy and Aunt Rose Leffler's golden wedding anniversary and Wallace and Iris [Leffler] had open house for them in their home in Madison. Several of the Leffler relatives came from Oklahoma and Iowa. We had them all in our home for noon dinner before going to Wallace's home. There were 30 or 40 of us. Some stayed a few days.

Ray flew to Kansas City in September and Bill Gist met him there and took him to Wheatland to visit his brother Charlie who was very ill. Uncle Fred McCracken stayed with me while he was gone.

December 5 we received a message from Myrtle that my brother Ira in Arlington, Washington, had suddenly died with a heart attack while doing chores on his dairy farm. Ethel, Raymond [Brown] and I went to the funeral. We went by bus to Aberdeen then via train to Seattle. This was a very scenic train ride. I was lucky and got to sit by the window all the way. My travelling companion was a lady from Minneapolis who was going to Seattle to visit her daughter. She cringed and covered her eyes every time she looked out the window. She had been a widow for two years and was the most forlorn unhappy woman I ever met. She confided that she hoped to find a man to marry in Seattle. I wondered how she ever got one much less two.

Ted from California and Kent from Idaho had already arrived at Ira's and met us in Seattle. It was a sad funeral for us all. Ira was the youngest of us Leffler children and was always so fun loving, his death seemed unreal. Kent was there in his pick up so Ethel, Raymond and I rode with him back to his home in Fruitland, Idaho. We were kind of squeezed into the seat but made it OK. While crossing the Cascade Mountains it snowed and Kent had to put on tire chains. Snow wasn't anything new to me but the scenic beauty it created in the mountains was a picture I'll always remember. We stayed at Kent's 3 days enjoying every minute with the family then took the train to Omaha then bus to Sioux Falls. Ray met me there and I was mighty glad to get home.

NOTES

1. Gilbert Fite suggests a similar scenario in *American Farmers: The New Minority* (Bloomington: Indiana Univ. Press), 117.

2. Between 1915 and 1930, the mines around Picher, Oklahoma, produced 50 percent of the world's supply of zinc. Although the industry went into decline in the 1930s, a minor boom occurred during World War II. During the years after the war, however, the mines closed. John W. Morris, *Ghost Towns of Oklahoma* (Norman: Univ. of Oklahoma Press, 1977), 147–49.

3. Although in 1948 there were still 221,000 horses and mules on South Dakota farms, ten years later there were only 67,000, according to the *Annual Report of the South Dakota Department of Agriculture, 1958* (Pierre: State of South Dakota, 1958), 120.

4. The small, kerosene-run Delco electric plants could power water pumps and, according to a 1920 advertisement aimed at farmers, would "make the home, the barn or the barnyard bright as day, at the touch of a button." Katherine Jellison, "Women and Technology on the Great Plains, 1900–1940," *Great Plains Quarterly* 8 (Summer 1988): 155.

5. Edith Ingalls graduated from Bryant High School in 1944, then as a sixteen-year-old began teaching country school during the school year and attending General Beadle College during the summer. She taught first grade in Watertown, South Dakota, the year before her wedding. After moving to the Pacific Northwest, she earned her bachelor's degree, taught for another sixteen years, and formed a tax return preparation business with Kent.

6. The "GI Bill of Rights," passed in April 1944, granted veterans a number of benefits, including $500 per year in tuition and monthly subsistence support ($50 per month, per veteran, plus $25 for dependents) for education; low-interest loans of up to $1,000 for housing; unemployment insurance; and medical aid in dozens of new Veterans' Administration hospitals. During the next two decades, 7 million veterans borrowed $66 billion in home loans; 10 million received $20 billion for schooling. Time Magazine, *Time Capsule: 1944* (New York: Time-Life Books, 1967), 24–25.

7. Most fowl are susceptible to some form of "fowlpox," which, like chicken pox, causes blisters to break out and scab over. Although the disease is not generally dangerous to the lives of chickens, experts advised against exposing chickens within four weeks of their first laying period, according to the U.S.

Department of Agriculture, *Animal Disease: Yearbook of Agriculture, 1956* (Washington, D.C.: U.S. Government Printing Office, 1956), 464–65.

8. Farmers had no way to prevent the growth of crop-damaging weeds until 1944, when 2-4-D, the first effective, safe herbicide, was marketed. The herbicide industry rapidly proliferated after the war. U.S. Department of Agriculture, *After a Hundred Years: Yearbook of Agriculture, 1962* (Washington, D.C.: U.S. Government Printing Office, 1962), 124–28.

9. By 1949, returning veterans had pushed enrollment at USD up to 1,768. The university, with help from the federal government, set up "Vets' Villa," a mobile home park to be occupied by veterans and their families; private owners of trailers could use spaces provided by the city in Austin Park. Cedric Cummins, *University of South Dakota, 1862–1966* (Vermillion: Dakota Press, 1975), 245–46.

10. Sara graduated from Fruitland High School and attended Idaho State University. She managed the Alaska Buyers Service for several years and now lives in Sacramento, California, with her husband Roger Young and their son Dane.

11. The artificial insemination of dairy cattle in the United States was well-established by the late 1930s; by 1946, artificial insemination was used by nearly 340 dairy cattle breeders, representing ownership of nearly 580,000 cows. This, of course, allowed more cows to be bred by fewer bulls. U.S. Department of Agriculture, *Science in Farming: Yearbook of Agriculture, 1943–1947* (Washington, D.C.: U.S. Government Printing Office, 1947), 113.

12. The White River Badlands became a National Monument in 1939. Lt. Col. George A. Custer described the area—frequently used by Indians as a haven from pursuing troops—as "Hell with the fires burned out," and the architect Frank Lloyd Wright marveled at the "sublime shapes" that inspired observers to commune with God. In the twentieth century the Badlands have offered scientists peeks into pre-history, with large concentrations of prehistoric fossils. Paul Putz, ed., *Historic Sites of South Dakota: A Guidebook* (Vermillion: Business Research Bureau, Univ. of South Dakota and Historical Preservation Center, 1980), 97.

13. A "cowboy orchestra" of a life-sized fiddler, mandolinist, guitarist, accordionist, spectator, and flea-scratching dog is one of the attractions at the famous Wall Drug, just east of the Black Hills. Founded in the early 1930s by Ted Hustead, Wall Drug's initial promise of free ice water has expanded to include dozens of shops, western art galleries, and a restaurant. A million people visit the store every year. For an entertaining pictorial account of the store, see Dana Close Jennings, *Free Ice Water! The Story of Wall Drug* (Aberdeen, S.Dak.: North Plains Press, 1969).

14. The Department of the Interior's fish hatchery near Spearfish began hatching trout to stock South Dakota streams in 1898 and is still in operation, according to Jennings, 115.

15. Named after a former businessman and mayor of Chicago, Garrett Biblical Institute opened in Evanston, Illinois, in 1855. Its founders hoped to supply Methodist ministers for the great American West, just then beginning to be settled. Almost from the beginning, a close relationship developed between the seminary and its neighbor, Northwestern University. After trying times dur-

ing the 1930s depression, Garrett recovered after the Second World War with a healthy influx of returning veterans.

A former professor at the seminary recalled that conflicts frequently arose between the veterans and wartime conscientious objectors at the school. Like Rodney, many of the students at Garrett worked at parishes while they went to school, sometimes commuting hundreds of miles. See Frederick A. Norwood, *From Dawn to Midday at Garrett* (Evanston, Ill.: Garrett-Evangelical Theological Seminary, 1978), 2–19, 42–43, 150, 151–52; Murray and Dorothy Leiffer, *Enter the Old Portals: Reminiscences—Fifty Years on a Seminary Campus* (Evanston, Ill.: Bureau of Social and Religious Research, 1987), 92–93.

16. Although the Korean War had erupted less than three months before, the South Dakota State Fair opened on September 4 in Huron. Good weather encouraged large crowds to attend the Labor Day "Thrill Day" program and the "1950 State Fair Review." Other displays included the South Dakota School of Mines and Technology's demonstration of making molasses from wood and the state safety department's display of photographs of car wrecks. This information is from the *Sioux Falls Daily Argus Leader,* September 5, 1950.

17. Beginning in 1936, the Rural Electrification Administration loaned money to local cooperatives to bring electricity to rural America. For a $5.00 deposit and less than $2.00 a month, farm families could enjoy electric lights, a radio, and the use of one other appliance—often an iron. By 1939, 25 percent of all farms in the United States had electricity. D. Clayton Brown, *Electricity for Rural America: The Fight for the REA* (Westport, Conn.: Greenwood Press, 1980), 67–75. Ray had paid a $5 membership fee to the local REA in 1950, although electricity was not provided to his farm for nearly two years.

18. Deadwood's Main Street and most of the town's businesses occupy the bottom of Deadwood Gulch. Houses climb the hills, slanting steeply up from the gulch, and the residential streets form terraces. See Federal Writers' Project of the Works Progress Administration, State of South Dakota, *A South Dakota Guide* (Pierre: State Publishing Co., 1938), 103–105.

19. Built before World War II, the Puget Sound Navy Yard at Bremerton employed 36,000 workers during the war, and the population of the city soared from 15,000 to 75,000 by 1944. Robert E. Fricken and Charles P. LeWarne, *Washington: A Centennial History* (Seattle: Univ. of Washington Press, 1988), 92, 132.

20. Begun in 1934, Grand Coulee Dam was completed in 1941 with help from New Deal programs. It dammed the Columbia River in northeastern Washington and was, according to one observer, "the biggest thing on earth." It provided electricity for much of the Pacific Northwest and irrigated the arid plain of eastern Washington (Fricken and LeWarne, 119–22).

21. Melissa graduated from Fruitland High School and received a degree in marketing at Boise State University. After working as finance director for the state Republican Party, she married Randy Nelson in 1979. They have a son named Tyler Ray. Melissa has been Executive Director of the Idaho Society of Public Accountants since 1979, and Randy works for a taxpayers' organization.

22. These purchases reflected the Gists' burgeoning prosperity. The rug cost nearly $170, and the vacuum cost more than $80.

23. Gladys recorded in the 1953 account book a $100 car loan to Rodney.

24. Doris Leivestad grew up in Inwood, Iowa, and graduated with a music degree and as valedictorian of her class of 1951 at Morningside College in Sioux City, Iowa. She taught at Soldier, Iowa, for the two years before she married Rodney and in the Canistota Public Schools from 1965 to 1968. She has also given piano lessons since 1969. Doris received her master's degree in Music Education from Black Hills State College in Spearfish, South Dakota, in 1972.

25. Howes Chapel was dedicated in 1952. Including the balcony, its seating capacity is an even hundred. The chapel has many stained glass windows with biblical and historical themes; its chancel windows proclaimed "Come, learn, go." A large organ, constructed by its donor, and a pulpit and lectern donated by alumni completed the intimate surroundings in which Rod and Doris were married. This was reported in Norwood, *From Dawn to Midday at Garrett,* 161–62.

26. Robert R. Spencer was born in Houghton, South Dakota, in 1925. After service as a paratrooper in World War II, he graduated from the University of South Dakota Law School and opened a practice in Madison. He served as Lake County States Attorney and as Madison city attorney. He retired because of ill health in 1981 and died five years later.

27. The WPA Guide to Utah called the two city blocks comprising Temple Square "the most visited point of interest in Utah." It includes the six-spired Temple of the Church of Jesus Christ of Latter-Day Saints (built between 1853 and 1893), the Tabernacle (auditorium), Assembly Hall, statues of Joseph and Hyrum Smith, a number of historic homes and buildings, and monuments to, among other things, the seagulls that saved the Mormon settlement from a cricket infestation in 1846. See Utah Writers' Project, Works Progress Administration, *Utah: A Guide to the State* (New York: Hastings House, 1941), 234–45.

28. A distant relative who eventually published extensive genealogies of the various branches of the Gist family in America.

29. Barbara graduated from Spearfish High School and from Morningside College. After divinity school at Vanderbilt University in Nashville, she served as a Methodist minister in Mobridge and Watertown, South Dakota, and then as campus pastor at Dakota Wesleyan University at Mitchell. In 1988 she began work toward a Ph.D. in church history at the University of Chicago.

30. By 1955, 42 percent of all farm families owned television sets; the average American household viewed television nearly five hours every day (Bogart, *Age of Television,* 17, 64). According to the program listings in the *Daily Leader* for July 15, 1955, residents of Madison could view only one station— KELO, out of Sioux Falls. Programming began at noon on Sundays, and at 10 A.M. on weekdays, and included the familiar mix of soap operas, variety and game shows, sports, cartoons, and westerns.

31. As late as 1948, less than half (45.5 percent) of all farms in the United States had a kitchen sink with running water; only 28.2 percent had bathtubs or showers. U.S. Bureau of the Census, *Statistical Abstract of the United States, 1950* (Washington, D.C.: U.S. Government Printing Office, 1950), 736.

32. John graduated from Fruitland High School and received his bachelor's degree from Boise State University. He has worked in agriculture, carpentry, forestry, and in nursing homes, but has for several years been a high school and junior high music teacher. He married Debra Frye, a nurse, in 1976, and they

have two children, Melody Jo, born in 1980, and Jed Raymond, born in 1985.

33. Linda graduated from Spearfish High School and from South Dakota State University with a degree in music. After teaching vocal music in Dunlap, Iowa, she trained to become a piano technician and tuner. She and her husband, James Marten, moved to Milwaukee, Wisconsin, in 1986, where she is a self-employed piano technician and he is a history professor at Marquette University. Their daughter Lauren was born in 1984 and their son Eli in 1992.

34. A meeting of "Free Soilers" met in Ripon in early 1854 to protest the Kansas-Nebraska Act, which made it possible for slavery to be extended into western territories. The Ripon meeting, one of many around the northern states, called for the creation of a "great Northern party," and named it the Republican Party. Richard N. Current, *The History of Wisconsin: The Civil War Era, 1848–1873* (Madison: State Historical Society of Wisconsin, 1976), 218–19.

35. Begun as Grove Manufacturing Company in 1903 to manufacture crude overalls, Oshkosh B'Gosh, Inc., grew into a worldwide organization famed for its "Oshkosh B'Gosh" overalls and children's wear. *Oshkosh: One Hundred Years a City, 1853–1953* (Oshkosh, Wisc.: Castle-Pierce Printing Co., 1953), 250.

36. From 1911 to 1966, Americans living in communities without banks could deposit their money in a nationwide system of savings accounts in post offices. Glenn G. Munn, *Encyclopedia of Banking & Commerce, 8th ed.* (Boston: Bankers Publishing Co., 1983), 770.

37. Oahe, the largest of the Pick-Sloan Plan's rolled-earth dams on the Missouri River, was begun in 1948 and completed in 1964; it created a 250-mile-long reservoir. Herbert Schell, *History of South Dakota,* 3d ed. (Lincoln: Univ. of Nebraska Press, 1975), 306.

38. Kirby graduated from Madison High School and then spent four years in the Air Force. After working for a few years in the Duval Copper Mine in Tucson, Arizona, he graduated as an electrical engineer from the University of Arizona in 1987. He is a lead project engineer for COMARCO in Sierra Vista, Arizona, and married Elizabeth Gray, a nurse, in 1991.

39. In 1960, 61.5 percent of South Dakotans had complete, working plumbing facilities. United States Bureau of the Census, *Statistical Abstract of the United States, 1964* (Washington, D.C.: U.S. Government Printing Office, 1964), 756.

GLADYS AND RAY
ON THEIR FORTY-FIFTH
WEDDING ANNIVERSARY, 1966.

THAT WONDERFUL PEACE, 1960–1971

After struggling on for a few more years, Ray's ever-worsening health forced him and Gladys to give up farming and move into Madison in the spring of 1964. Gladys missed her flower garden but seemed to enjoy the convenience of town-life and kept in touch with her old neighbors. There were short walks and country drives, and even a few trips to visit relatives out of state. This peaceful, urban interlude together lasted only three years; Ray finally died in April 1967.

The daily diaries Gladys kept from the mid-1960s into the 1970s reveal how she coped with the loss of her partner of nearly half a century. Seven years after his death, she wrote, "The loneliness still aches," and contemporary events occasionally awakened memories of experiences with Ray. She remained typically practical, however. Once, she discovered that pigeon grass had overgrown the bluegrass she had sown on his grave. "He spent his life plowing out pigeon grass," she vowed testily, "I'm *not* going to leave it there."

Gladys was wracked but not overcome with grief. She sought comfort, as she had all her life, in family and friends, with children and grandchildren meeting her emotional needs, as her father had done years before. In her diaries she often commented about card games and potluck suppers with the other "porch rockers" in the neighborhood. She also widened her own horizons and experiences, while at the same time fulfilling some old ambitions. She flew in a jet, toured California, and enjoyed seeing her seven grandchildren grow and prosper, especially Lee and Kirby Spencer, who lived nearby and visited often. Most of them received college degrees—which was nearly unheard of for family members of Ray's and Gladys's generation—and then eventually matured and scattered, as Gists and Lefflers had done for decades, even centuries, building homes in places ranging from the Great Lakes to the Pacific Northwest to the desert Southwest.

Gladys also pursued her interests in history and music. She continued to compile genealogical information, finished her reminiscences, and completed a history of the Methodist Church in Madison. She took up the violin, climbing several flights of stairs once every week for lessons from a professor at Dakota State College. "At least it's not a Government Senior Citizen project. . . . I'm paying for it myself," wrote the adamantly Republican seventy-year-old. She loved to be asked to play for visitors to the little pink house on Center Street, and she occasionally performed for audiences at the old church in Prairie Village, an outdoor museum west of Madison. Gladys sometimes served as hostess to school groups in the church, when she would relate the history of the building and sometimes lead sing-a-longs of old hymns. In 1977 Gladys reigned as "Pioneer Queen" of the annual threshing jamboree at Prairie Village; she proudly sported a crown and banner and waved to crowds from a restored 1924 Dodge that reminded her of the car that had carried her little family to Presho fifty years before. Prairie Village must have served as a bittersweet reminder to Gladys of her own experiences on the prairie; it certainly provided her with activities to fill her days and acted as a bridge between her past and present.

1 9 6 0

In January we traded our dark green 1950 Packard car in on a 1957 ivory and blue Ford Fairlane. We had driven the Packard for ten years and we have never had a car that we liked so well and derived so much pleasure from. The Ford was lighter and I almost had to learn to drive again.

Ray's brother Charlie was buried February 1st and Rodney and Ray drove our new (to us) car to Wheatland, Missouri, to attend the funeral. I stayed home to attend the fires and chores. It was cold but they had a quick good trip.

Ray's health was failing and he could not stand so much hard work any more so we sold all livestock and only kept a few chickens. We sure missed the cattle. This was the last year that we farmed the two quarters of land. Mr Sponholtz rented one quarter to Leonard Olson, our nearest neighbor. We hired quite a little help during the summer. Albert Crawford ran the corn picker in the fall and Gary Olson helped Ray unload.

I raised fewer pullets and kept a smaller flock of hens. We raised 100 cockerels and when they were ready Ruth's and Rodney's families came out and we butchered them all and divided them for our freezers.

We splurged a little for our comfort in September. We went shopping and bought a new davenport and two Barca lounger chairs. It was the first new upholstered furniture we ever had. We never had anything that we used in sheer comfort as much as those two chairs.

During corn picking in October I discovered a lump on the left side of my spine and it nearly scared me to death. The Doctor thought it was a growth on the kidney. It didn't show on Xrays so he performed surgery and discovered it was muscle. I had injured my spine sometime and the muscle was nature's way of cushioning it.

1 9 6 1

This year started out to be easier as caring for 200 hens was
all the chores we had to do. Ray only farmed one quarter of
land which was enough as his emphysema was getting worse.
He was tired all the time and plagued with throat troubles. He
was 68 years old March 25 and started taking his social security insurance of $109 per month which helped us to hire some
help.

When school was out Kent's family came from Idaho for
a two weeks' visit. While they were here, Ruth, Edith and the
club I belonged to planned and gave us an open house celebration in our home June 8 for our 40th wedding anniversary.
Marion and Evalyn Gist from Yucaipa, California, were here
visiting and they prolonged their visit to be with us. June 7,
Marion & Evalyn and us went to Sioux Falls shopping and I
got a new navy blue crepe dress for the event. June 8 was on
a Sunday and it was a much remembered day for us. Our
family all attended church in a group and we were humbly
grateful to be so honored. And so proud of them. The folks
from Inwood all came up and the McCracken [and] Leffler
families then enjoyed a picnic dinner in the Junius school[1]
then we went home and received guests thru the afternoon
and evening. Rodney was in Rapid City to [South Dakota
Methodist A]nnual [C]onference and drove about all night to
get back to be with us.

We spent the afternoon and evening receiving guests at
home. The girls had the house all fixed up nice and a beautiful table with a wedding cake, and flowers in Mrs. Hexom's
epergne. They served a picnic supper to several of the guests
on the lawn. Uncle Leonard McCracken and Omer Hunt were
there from Wheatland, Missouri. Wally [Leffler] took a lot of
pictures. We treasure the many cards and gifts and thoughtful-
ness of our dearest friends.

As soon as Ray got the fall plowing done we decided to
take a trip to Illinois and visit Monts. On September 22 we

drove to Greene, Iowa, and visited Ernest and Marian Gist
overnight. After a pleasant visit we left the next morning in a
drizzly rain. We lunched in Iowa City and rested awhile then
started on and about 5 miles south, as we were going up a wet
hill, two young men passed another [car] and came over the
crest in our traffic lane and we had a bad collision. No one
was killed but one young man was badly cut about his head
and face. We were not thrown out of our car but thrown forward and badly stunned. Ray had a broken right . . . wrist
and I a broken left hip in the socket joint. An ambulance
took us to the Iowa City hospital on a Saturday afternoon.
Many of the doctors and staff were gone so it took a long
time before we were taken care of. It was nearly midnight
before we were finally put to bed in 40-bed wards after Xrays,
etc. Ray's arm was a bad break, they set it twice and never
did get it right, it healed crooked with 30% disability. We were
in different wards so we could only lie and worry about each
other in a completely strange place.

I telephoned Mont and Ruth while lying on a stretcher
but asked them not to come at once as we were not critical.
Mont was nearer so came the next morning. We stayed in
Iowa City hospital three days keeping in touch with the children by phone, then Mont made an ambulance of his station
wagon and he and Rena brought us home to Madison —
transferred me to hospital here and Ray was able to go home.
I lay in the hospital for 30 days then home on crutches for 6
weeks. I could use crutches like an elephant. Bill and Doris
Gist came while I was in the hospital and spent a week helping Ray. Ruth did the laundry and cleaning. Ray's arm was
still in a cast when I went home. Our wonderful neighbor
women said "don't worry about a thing," and every day for
two weeks one of them came as they planned, brought our
dinner and supper at noon and set it on the table. By that
time Ray got the cast off his arm and I was stronger so we
managed our work fine. We were amply covered by insurance
so was not hurt financially. Bob helped us with all of that.

We did not see our blue car again it was sold for salvage.

When we first got home Jack Gist brought a 1958 Ford out
for Ray to drive and as soon as we were able to be around we
bought it. I am still driving it now in 1968.

1 9 6 2

We spent a quiet winter at home in 1962. No chores to do so
we just got out for shopping, church and a few social
visits when weather was nice.

On June 1st Bob brought Kirby out to stay with us a few
days and announced that Lee Robert Spencer had just arrived.[2] Now Grandpa had two grandsons near by to fuss over.
But Kirby could walk and talk so got the most attention until
Lee grew big enough.

Ray was able to do the farming except for some machine
hire and a man during corn picking.

As soon as he finished fall plowing we again started for
Monts in Illinois and this time we had a delightful trip. It was
October and we drove a few miles down the Mississippi River.
The autumn coloring of foliage was beautiful. Mont and Rena
took us on some long scenic drives and we enjoyed every minute of it. The men recognized the different kinds of trees.
Pecan, oak, maple, etc. A tree was a tree to me. I marveled at
the colors. I picked up some large acorns and brought [them]
home and some hedge apples which Ray made me eventually
burn. He wasn't about to risk any seed growing in South Dakota. They were pretty in table arrangements. I was going
through a "phase" of dried arrangements and of preserving
flowers in borax. One year I worked on a church committee
and we sold $130 worth of centerpieces at our WSCS bazaar. I
wondered what words a farmer would utter when he found his
wife had paid good money for dried weeds.

My garden was now mostly flowers, all kinds of them,

not exactly landscaped but blooming in profusion in [the]
most unlikely spots. Ray had lots of patience to help me haul
all kinds of roots, slips and bulbs home to try. When Aunt
Rose Leffler and I visited Ray and Emmett said they might as
well put a spade and a box in the back of the car. When we
moved off the farm in 1964 many of the neighbors commented
on how they missed my flower garden when they drove past.
The first year it grew wild and full of weeds and was mowed
off eventually.

1 9 6 3

In April I had an attack of flu or something. I fainted every
time I sat up. Ray took me to the doctor and from there to
the hospital. I recovered quickly and in three days was ready
to go home. When Ray came after me he had a terrible cold
and the doctor advised him to stay in the hospital. He took
me home and when I phoned Ruth about it she talked to Dr.
Whitson and phoned us she would be right out to take her
Dad to hospital and me home with her. After two days there I
was able to go home in daytime. Ray had made arrangements
for Oscar W. Olson to work for us so he came each day and
put in our 60 A. of oats. Ray had pneumonia and by the time
he got home Oscar had the grain all in.

Oscar did about all of our farming that year except Ray
ran the two row corn picker in the fall. Ray's emphysema was
getting gradually worse and any exertion left him exhausted.
The doctor warned repeatedly about smoking and he tried
hard to quit but couldn't seem to shake the habit. Our medical bills were increasing every year.[3]

[*Rodney recalled that Ray rolled his own cigarettes for
many years, then smoked Camels. Prodded by Gladys's disap-
proval, he often snuck into the barn to smoke, until Gladys*

declared, "If you're going to smoke, you're going to smoke in the house!"]

In August we put a lock on our doors (the first time they were ever locked), sold all of our hens and went via train to visit Kents again. We left our car with Ruth and she took us to Sioux Falls to catch the bus to Omaha, then we rode the U[nion] P[acific] train to Ontario. We had a good trip and enjoyed Kent's family so much.

Two days after we got home the phone rang and Bill Gist said he and Joe Gist and their wives would soon be there. I felt like anything but company but welcomed them. The next day Bill asked us to go to Huron to the fair with them so we did but Ray had had all the traveling he needed. He couldn't do much walking at the fair and it started to rain in the P.M. so we went on west to Pierre to see the capitol.[4] It poured rain while [we] were there about an hour then we went to Presho and took a motel for the night.

Bill was anxious to look up some of his old friends around Presho but the roads were so muddy we dared not get off the paving. We knew what that gumbo mud was. We made a few telephone calls after breakfast, stopped at Harold Brakke's on [the] hiway and in Reliance to see Rachael (Stevens) then on home where I cooked them a good ham dinner.

We had our local club Christmas party in December. Benora Hexom and I decorated the house and everybody brought food. Then it *STORMED*. A real South Dakota blizzard. Seven couples came and we made merry until about midnight. It was no night to be on the roads they could hardly see even where the road was. We kept the telephones ringing until everybody got home. Clarence and Doris Rongley had to walk the last few rods in snow above their knees. That was our last stormy night party.

1 9 6 4

Ray's health kept gradually failing. In February he couldn't get out of the house and it was an effort to get around inside. He did not have sharp pain but emphysema of lungs left him exhausted from any physical activity. On February 23 he collapsed in his chair with labored breathing. I called the ambulance and asked for oxygen. It had to come the 7 miles in the country and I thought it would never get there. They lifted him on a stretcher and rushed to the hospital. I followed in our car.

Ruth and Rodney were both away from home so I did not leave Ray's bedside long enough to try to locate them but our minister Ronald Hartung came and located them both by phone. They came at once and our doctor advised sending for Kent; he flew to Sioux Falls arriving the next day. Ray got slowly better and after 16 days in hospital we took him home. Kent stayed a week and while the family were all here we decided it would be better for us to leave the farm so we shopped around for a home in Madison and bought our two bedroom pink house on 532 E. Center Street for $8250. Having had a little auction training, Kent helped me make the preliminary arrangements for an auction sale before he went home. [*On the day that Ray and Gladys put down $500 on their new home, Gladys wrote in her diary, "So we are committed to a house. The first one we have ever owned and I expect the only one."*]

We could not get possession of our new home before April 1st so I took Ray back to the farm and I was more than busy caring for him, getting ready to move and for the sale. I was so thankful to have him to manage and to talk things over with.

Our wonderful neighbors came with their pick up trucks and moved us to our new home March 31 and the next day they came and had everything lined up and ready for the auction sale by noon. Bill and Doris Gist came from Kansas City;

[they] were such good help and comfort and of course Rodney and Ruth were as busy as I was. Rodney brought his Dad out to the farm in the afternoon while the auctioneer was selling, but he was unable to get out of the car.

We bought a 25 lb portable oxygen outfit and I learned how to administer it when the emphysema spasms came and Ray finally conquered the smoking habit. His health slowly improved and he got able to be around the home and drive the car so we enjoyed this year in our new home getting it fixed up to suit our taste.

We had new railing put on our front porch and a new aluminum screen door and did some painting. We put down new carpeting, drapes and did general cleaning. It was fun to see what shrubs and flowers emerged around the house in the spring. For the first time I had no garden to plant or tend. Occasionally we drove out around the farm but strangely enough it did not seem like home — because there was nothing or no one that we loved there. The fields looked familiar and sometimes we felt a deep nostalgia for the intimacy with the good earth and growing crops and harvest.

There were three college boys rooming in a basement room of our house when we bought it. They wanted to stay until school was out so we let them. They did not bother us much but they were very *un-neat* and not the best therapy for a sick man.

PUBLIC AUCTION SALE

Because of poor health I will sell the following located 5 miles east of Madison, S. D. on Highway 34, 2 north and ½ east; or west of Wentworth, S. D., to the roadside park, 2 miles north and ½ east, on

WEDNESDAY, APRIL 1 — 1:00 P.M.

MACHINERY — 1951 Allis Chalmers tractor with Comfort cover; 1942 Farmall tractor; 1950 Case A-6 combine, 4-row Allis-Chalmers cultivator; 4-row Oliver corn planter; IHC side delivery rake; M.M. 2-row corn picker; J.D. 10-foot binder-windrower; Farmhand loader, wide bucket; shotgun seeder; 16-foot auger with motor; good fanning mill; J.D. 15-foot disc; 7-foot IHC power mower; 4-section flexible drag; 2 2-bot. 16-in. plows; IHC manure spreader, 4-wheel, on rubber; Wards 6-h.p. engine; 36-foot elevator with jack; 2 factory wagons with hoists; IHC 10-foot grain binder; 2 discs, IHC and Ford; IHC 7-foot power mower; J.D. side delivery rake, on steel; New Idea manure spreader; steel wheel wagon with flatbed; IHC 2-row corn planter on steel; wood wheel running gear and wood box; factory built running gear and box; factory trailer and wood flare box; grain elevator, narrow carriage; corn picker; 8x14 flatbed.

MISCELLANEOUS — Air compressor (nearly new; water tanks and heaters; feed bunk; M.M. hammermill; several rolls slat-cribbing; chicken nests and feeders; 2 wood wheel wagons; bench vise and anvil; 300-gallon gas tank and stand; endless belts; buzz saw; lots of scrap metal; horse drawn machinery; old harness; hand tools.

BUILDINGS — 10x12 Brooder house; bottle gas brooder
FEW BALES STRAW IN BARN

HOUSEHOLD GOODS—Cedar lined wardrobe; Kimball upright piano; 2 Aladdin lamps; kerosene lamps and other miscellaneous household goods.

J. R. GIST, OWNER

VERNELL JOHNSON AND CURTIS PRICE, AUCTIONEERS.
SECURITY BANK, CLERK.

AUCTION NOTICE,
Madison Daily Leader, MARCH 26, 1964.
(REPRINTED WITH PERMISSION OF THE *Madison Daily Leader*.)

1 9 6 5

We spent a comfortable winter with the warm insulated house and automatic gas heat we had to look outside to know that it was winter. I kept attending the Co-workers club of our farm neighbor women and my church work. Sometimes Ray was able to attend church with me. Our part of town was mostly retired people and we had very good neighbors.[5]

In April we spent a week with Rodney's girls in Canistota while they took a little vacation trip.

In July Bill Gist phoned that his father Fred Gist, Ray's older brother, had passed away. Ray wanted to go, so after he went to his doctor for a health check we left that same afternoon. We drove to Inwood that eve[ning] for overnight at Ethel's then on to Wheatland the next day. We took turns driving and made good time 600 miles. We stopped at Jim Marshall's in Kansas City for an hour of relaxation and rest and arrived at Wheatland about 8 P.M. A lot of relatives were there and we were made welcome in Oral Gist's lovely home. We were tired and relaxed a while the next day then mingled with relatives in Bill's home. Some of them I had never met and Ray had not seen them for years.

The funeral was the next day and it was extremely hot uncomfortable weather. I think there are more than twenty Gist graves in the Gardner cemetery south of Wheatland. Ray's parents and grandmother Elizabeth Gist are buried there. The most of the relatives left soon after the funeral but we stayed for two weeks visiting old friends and relatives. One day we drove to Springfield, Missouri, and called on his sister Edna's children (Homer and Grace) then on to Mt. Vernon to visit my Aunt Adda Paris, 84 years old. She is my favorite Aunt, so much like my father. I wish I could be with her often.

While in Wheatland one night we received a telephone call from Raymond that their only son Lloyd's sickness was diagnosed as terminal cancer and he was very ill, so we hurried home to be near them in their sorrow. Lloyd was in the [Veterans' Administration] hospital in Sioux Falls and lived for over a month longer, just wasting away. We made some trips from home to Inwood to be with the family there. Opal came home from California to be with her parents. Lloyd's death was August 26, 1965, and that night when I called Kent in Fruitland, Idaho, to tell him about it we found Kent in the hospital there to have major surgery for kidney stones.

We kept in touch with them via phone and decided to go to Idaho via train to be with him when he came home from the hospital as Edith was teaching and their children all in school. Were we surprised when he met us at the train! He couldn't move very fast but was up and around some. The children had grown so much and we were so happy to see them all. We stayed three weeks and helped them all we could until Kent could work again and felt good.

Their orchard was full of beautiful ripe apples and Grandpa really enjoyed walking among the trees.

We took our 25 lb. oxygen bottle along on all of our travels but were fortunate not to have to use it. The trip coming home was very tiring for Ray especially the change from train to bus in Omaha. Ruth met us in Sioux Falls and we were mighty glad to get home.

We had left our car for Doris to drive to school in Sioux Falls while we were gone. They were living in Canistota and she was taking a refresher course in Sioux Falls College. After we got back they bought a second car. Most families were two car families or more now. It seemed like all families needed two salaries to live on. A generation on the run. Chasing Rainbows. Working for more education, more entertainment, more of everything. I guess people have been like that ever since Adam and Eve. We just have more ways to run now and more rainbows to chase.

Mont and Rena came for a visit in October. It doesn't seem just right to start a winter without a visit with them one

way or another. We didn't do much driving around except for
short drives, just relaxed and enjoyed being together. We spent
½ a day seeing the start of Prairie Village west of Madison
and enjoyed the lake drives.[6]

1 9 6 6

This was a year for sickness and doctor bills for both of us.
While visiting at Kent's last September I had a severe spell
of nausea for a few days and the doctor advised me to have
gall bladder Xrays when I got home. I didn't do it until [in]
June another attack sent me to the hospital for a few days
and eventually, on July 23, I submitted to surgery and had [a]
gall bladder full of stones removed. Ray was feeling pretty
good then, so we both got along fine, and I recovered quickly.

During the last week in September we decided to take a
trip to Illinois to visit Mont and Rena. We stayed at Inwood
the first night then to Griswold, Iowa, for an overnight visit
with Eula and Joel Boone. Eula and I were inseparable chums
as teenagers. I hadn't seen her for years and found her to be
in poor health and she didn't seem to be very happy. They
welcomed us warmly and we enjoyed our visit with them very
much.

Ray was not in any pain but tired easily. We drove on to
Mont's the next day taking turns at driving and enjoying the
scenery. We took a drive along the Mississippi River south of
Burlington which we enjoyed much.

We did not do much tripping at Mont's as Ray rested a
lot. We did drive one P.M. to an old Indian burial mound
which has been excavated and restored for an interesting display. I don't see how they ever got those skeletons so carefully
uncovered, and taped descriptions given by ear phones of each
group as we stopped to look and listen.[7]

We avoided the main hiways on the way home, just took

a good road going in the right direction (following the map).

We stopped at Ernest Gist's in Greene, Iowa, one after-noon and found Marian not well with a bad cough so we took them down town for supper then stayed overnight and visited. Jean [*Ernest and Marian Gist's daughter*] has a charming fam-ily. They all came to see us.

Ray was pretty tired when we got home. This was the last vacation trip we had together and a precious memory to me.

The winter was not a severe one and we were comfortable except for worry about his health. He was not bedfast at any time and sometimes drove the car for errands and sat in it while I shopped. He seemed to be failing and I was anxious for spring to come so we could get out for a little more fresh air and exercise. On nice Sundays we went to church together but some times I don't think he felt like it. We drove out to Ruth's often and enjoyed the grandsons a lot. But he didn't have the strength to go for walks or play with them as he wanted to do.

1 9 6 7

Spring finally came and Ray decided to take a little walk every day, a block or two, with his cane, when weather was nice. The last part of April his back bothered him a lot and leg cramps were very painful. April 23 he decided to go to the doctor for back pain and he was sent right to the hospital for all kinds of Xrays and clinical tests. They put him in traction for a collapsed vertebra. Then the doctor decided to operate for prostate gland trouble. Ray had never had much trouble that we associated with that but he told the doctor to go ahead if necessary. Rodney, Ruth and I stood by during the surgery and stayed with him by turns until the next morning he got worse and we all stayed near as doctors and nurses

worked with him but he lost consciousness and passed away
about noon. The doctor disclosed to us then that the lab analysis proved the gland full of cancer which had spread.

Kent and Edith rushed home and several of Ray's relatives from away came. Brother Mont & Rena from Illinois
and nephews and nieces from Illinois and Missouri.

Our children, relatives, friends, so many helped [me] thru
the immediate shock. My brother Ted came from California
and stayed two weeks. What a comfort that was, as three days
after the funeral everybody else was gone. Ted and I went to
Inwood for a few days which was the last time my sister,
brother and I were together. When we came back Ted took the
plane from Sioux Falls for his home in California and I drove
on home alone.

When I came in the house and faced the empty chair and
the stillness I was overwhelmed with grief for awhile. How
could I live now without his love and companionship which I
had had for 46 years? But I knew that I must go on as Ray
would wish and that I must do it alone. I had spent very few
nights alone in my life. This was the first thing I had to accept. I shall always be grateful to my widowed friend Mary
Johnson who spent so many evenings helping me to adjust.
Ray left our business in perfect order so I did not have to
worry about how I was to live financially; if I could manage it
wisely I could live within my income.

But learning to make decisions for myself was another
thing I had to learn. One day when I was feeling especially
low a letter came in the mail from Jim Marshall, Ray's
nephew whom both of us admired and loved. He suggested
that I read Isaiah 41:10.

> Fear not, for I am with you,
> Be not dismayed, for I am the Lord your God;
> I will strengthen you with my victorious right hand.

How comforting the assurance! It sustained me thru many long
days and nights.

In December there was a letter from Ted and Edith that the

doctors had discovered a growth in his lung that was malignant, and inoperable. Edith was teaching and Ted had been retired from active work for some time because of arteriosclerosis and a heart condition. He was at home alone most days so I began to plan a trip to California.

1 9 6 8

I had never travelled alone but I decided to fly over the mountains, as it was winter, then try to see some new country and visit some relatives and friends that we had entertained many times, and spend some time with Ted. Lucky for me my friend Elsie Tupper wanted to go to Los Angeles and Seattle to visit her folks so we spent some pleasant hours planning and getting ready. It made the winter go faster. February 28 we boarded the plane in Sioux Falls for Phoenix where she visited her friends and I with Ernest Gists for two days. [*Two nights before she left for California, Gladys dreamed "of Ray going with me in a car. . . . Why did I have to wake up?" she asked her diary.*]

From Phoenix Elsie flew to L.A. to visit her son Gilbert and I went alone via bus to Yucaipa, California, to visit Ray's brother Marion and wife Evalyn. Marion met me at the station and when I saw that head of beautiful white hair so much like Ray's I nearly choked. Evalyn was not well and unable to be around much, but she was kind enough to let Marion take me for long sight-seeing drives for two days. Then I went on by bus to Encinitas for a week with Edgar Wattenbargers, old friends since childhood. From there up the coast by bus to Santa Paula to Ted's so I saw a lot of California. Ted and I had been separated during the most of our years of marriages and now grief and illness had brought us together again. We had both learned a lot from life and these two weeks were precious to us both.

I flew from L. A. to Boise and spent a month with Kent's family. They were all gone all day on school days but I was getting used to solitude and rather enjoyed it. There was plenty of life when they got home.

Elsie met me there and we came home together April 23 via train.

Home was good, lonely, but my refuge. If I can't have my loved one I'd rather live alone, surrounded by wonderful friends and family affection.

The summer went fast. July 3 I drove to Sioux Falls to see Rodney's family off to England for a year. They will be gone long and I will miss them but they were so excited and thrilled with anticipation that I was happy to see them so happy. [*Rod, Doris, Barb, and Linda lived in Louth, Lincoln-shire, from the summer of 1968 to the summer of 1969. Louth is an agricultural center of 12,000 people. The girls attended local schools and Rodney served several Methodist churches and "societies" in the Louth area.*]

I had always wanted to study more music and the only available instrument was the three violins which our family had inherited. In August I finally got up the courage to ask Mr. Lotspeich, one of the college professors, to help me. He surely had patience with me. It was the best therapy for lone-liness that I could find. I just loved it.

The snow came in December. Plenty of it. Just before Christmas I took my car out to Bob's and left it in their ga-rage. I didn't know I would miss it so much. They came after me Christmas eve and I spent the next day enjoying Santa Claus with their family until about four P.M. The snow was raging in a blizzard so Bob brought me home. My little house is so comfortable I have to go outside or listen to radio to know what [the] weather really is.

1 9 6 9

The snow continued, huge drifts and all traffic stopped several times for two or three days during the winter. [*The winter of 1968–69 was one of the most severe in recent South Dakota history. On January 1 the Sioux Falls Argus Leader reported that Gov. Frank Farrar had declared eastern South Dakota a disaster area. "Sub-zero temperatures and winds continued to battle man and machine to a virtual standstill," declared the state's largest newspaper. Fifty inches of snow covered the ground east of the Missouri River; hundreds of cattle had already frozen; and dozens of farm families were in need of emergency help."*]

I rented my basement bedroom to a college senior, Tom Orton, last September and he proved to be the best roomer I have had, more like my own family around and it helped the loneliness during the winter having someone come and go. He was a star basketball player so I listened to some games and when nothing to do I could take that old fiddle and get lost for an hour or two at a time. I always shut the door and windows so the neighbors couldn't hear the screeching.

Mary or Iome or both came over about every evening and we played scrabble. Ruth came after Mary and I for church so the winter went by and spring came. When the snow melted the countryside was flooded in many places. The creek ran over and lapped the sidewalk in front of my house and we had some anxious moments that it might flood the basement but it remained dry. I got my car home for Easter.

June 3 President Nixon and family visited Madison to dedicate our new Karl Mundt library. We all joined the huge crowd on the campus to see and hear him. It was the first time I had ever seen a United States President. Lee came home sparkling! *He* even shook hands with the President!

The years of 1967–68–69 were years when many youth rebelled against our Asiatic war in Viet Nam, and Dr. Martin Luther King was leading a racial movement to better the lives of Negroes. Marches and gatherings to promote their causes soon turned into the rape of cities with vandalism and murder. Millions of dollars worth of proprty and homes were destroyed. They seemed to be against everything and *for* nothing but to hate and destroy. Our peaceful little city of Madison was worried that such confusion might happen here when the President came but it was a beautiful day and the ceremony went as it was well planned.

In July Rodneys returned from England. They had enjoyed a very pleasant year of work, school and travel and were glad to be home again. They moved to Spearfish in August to begin work there.

I spent a week via bus in October with Mont and Rena. Rena was recovering from catarac [sic] surgery, Mont having back trouble and Toots in hospital for surgery, so we spent a quiet week of visiting. [*Rena "Toots" Parker was Fred Gist's daughter, who had lived with her uncle and aunt, Mont and Rena, while she was growing up.*]

The first part of November I spent a week with Rodney. Really enjoyed being with their family and touring the beautiful hills.

October 15, 1969. This is the day when America in various ways works for a moratorium on the Viet Nam war.[8] I pray for the Governments of all nations to find wisdom for people to live in peace. If each of us would keep the peace of God in our hearts there would be no wars. But I find myself in a perpetual struggle to keep that peace, because of the things I do or don't do. Countries are made up of people so the world is in eternal struggle. And when we cease to struggle — we are dead. Occasionally I catch a glimpse of that wonderful peace — when I have kept in tune with God. But I know that I can not just sit and revel in it for long, I must get up and get going and try to help someone else to find it for it is the most precious thing that I have found.

I talked myself (with the urging of a good salesman) into a new RCA color television for Christmas and altho I am not an avid television fan I really enjoyed it. Spent Christmas with Ruth's family and Rodney's came a few days later for a family Christmas. Stored my car at Bob's again for the winter.

1 9 7 1

November 28, 1971, the last of the Sponholtz family who owned the place we farmed for 19 years died. They were wealthy and Gilbert who had never married left a large estate which had been accumulated by the family. There were no family heirs other than aged cousins. When the estate notice was published in the paper I was astonished to see my name among the benefactors. I couldn't imagine what he had left to me as the "survivor of Ray and Gladys Gist." It must be his sister's piano which he knew I had sold when we left the farm because it was worn out and too large and heavy to fit into our little house. I was puzzled, but decided to just wait and see what developed.

Kent's family flew home from Idaho for Christmas and Rodney's family drove in from Spearfish on Christmas day and we all gathered in Ruth's beautiful home on Lake Herman to celebrate together. I missed Ray so much it hurt! But it was no time to sit around and mourn with all the love of our family around me. The activities in the kitchen, and around the sparkling big tree in the living room with all of the mystery and colorful packages around it. And the rosy cheeked snow mobilers hustling in and out to exchange into insulated costumes for comfort in the cold.

When dinner was ready we all gathered around the table and sang the traditional table grace "Joy to the World." In spite of the big lump in my throat it was one of the happiest days of my life. We enjoyed all of the Christmas goodies then after dinner the big event of gift opening with all of the Ohs and Ahs! There was a loving gift for Grandma from every loving child and grandchild. Bob presented me with a copy of the Sponholtz will and when I read these lines it was the shock of my life!! "I give, devise and bequeath to my good friend Gladys Gist, a life estate and interest to the S. E. ¼ of Section (30) township 107, Lake County, South Dakota, so long as she remains unmarried. She shall receive all the rents, issues and profits from said real property" etc. etc. Upon my death the property [was] to go to the West Center Street Baptist Church.

What a legacy from my husband, their father! We can be forever proud of his Christian ethics, and business relationship with all men regardless of monetary values!

NOTES

1. Junius, a hamlet located a few miles west of Madison, was known in its early years for its Saturday night dances; the town was nicknamed "Hollywood," reported Dale Jahr, in *Lake County Pictorial History* (Madison, S.Dak.: Prairie Historical Society, 1976), 12.

2. Lee Spencer graduated from Madison High School in 1980 and from the University of Montana in 1984, with a degree in forestry. He now lives in Ellensburg, Washington, and is employed by Plum Creek Timber Co. He is married to Kristin Stark, a registered nurse. A son, Ryan Robert, was born in 1990 and a daughter, Katie, was born in 1992.

3. The Gists' medical bills rose from $94.38 in 1959 to $616.32 in 1964. After a brief respite in 1965, the bills mounted to $1,874.99 in 1966. Insurance paid all but $352.80.

4. The neoclassical South Dakota state capitol was built of sandstone and limestone in 1912. Italian craftsmen laid a floor of Italian marble and Corinthian columns frame the grand staircase. Paul Putz, *Historic Sites of South Dakota* (Vermillion: Business Research Bureau, University of South Dakota, and Historical Preservation Center, 1990), 88.

5. Among their close neighbors were the editor's great-uncle and great-aunt, Bill and Annie Wesenberg.

6. A number of lakes — known as the "skunk lakes" to white traders and trappers early in the nineteenth century — dot the landscape near Madison, including Lake Herman, the largest, and Lakes Madison, Milwaukee, Long, Brandt, and Bradus. (Jahr, 4, 9). Prairie Village, perched on the shore of Lake Herman two miles west of Madison, is the site of dozens of restored and furnished buildings from the pioneer era. It grew out of an old-time threshing demonstration in 1961 (Putz, 75).

7. This was apparently Monks' Mound (named for the French monks who worked among the Indians), near Cahokia, which is the largest prehistoric earth work in North America. It totals 17 acres and is 100 feet high. It dates from the Middle Mississippian culture that flourished around A. D. 900. See Robert P. Howard, *Illinois: A History of the Prairie State* (Grand Rapids, Mich.: William B. Erdmans, 1972), 12.

8. The *Argus Leader* reported that the participation in the protest by students at South Dakota's colleges was "minimal and orderly." A few classes were called off at the University of South Dakota and only 300 to 400 students showed up at the rally held at South Dakota State University. At Dakota State in

Madison, 200 of the school's 1,300 students turned out to protest the war. Far more action occurred in other parts of the country; 90,000 people rallied on Boston Common, and thousands ringed the White House in a candlelight vigil. *Sioux Falls Argus Leader,* October 16, 1969.

GLADYS FIDDLING AT PRAIRIE VILLAGE.

EPILOGUE, 1975

1 9 7 5

This diary ends here. If any one wants to add the final chapter it won't take long. I have learned to live alone and have been blest with good health. There's a few diaries that Kent sent me to keep scattered around the house and kept spasmodically. All sound about alike. My material wants are few.

MOTHER.

Gladys died thirteen years after she wrote these last words of her reminiscences. Fragile and ever more forgetful, she had finally entered a Madison nursing home in September 1987. She continued to be active in her church and with her surviving friends, although she fretted because she could no longer serve them coffee and cookies as she had, with considerable pride, countless times in her life. She thought sometimes of playing her violin, but arthritis prevented her from entertaining visitors. On Christmas Eve 1988 she suffered a severe stroke and never regained full consciousness. A few days later she slipped peacefully away.

Mourners at her funeral sang the same hymns they had sung at Ray's: "Love Divine and Love's Excelling" and "O Love That Wilt Not Let Me Go." The third verse of the latter goes:

O Joy that seekest me through pain,
I cannot close my heart to thee;
I trace the rainbow through the rain,
And feel the promise is not vain,
that morn shall tearless be.

Gladys reached the ends of many rainbows during her nearly ninety years: a long, happy marriage; healthy, prosperous children; and, after many struggles, modest financial security. She had not chased her rainbows blindly or recklessly, but had followed them with religious faith, determination, and a confidence that things would work out all right.

When she was eighty, Gladys wrote, "At this stage in life one learns to live in the present." Still, she believed that "we have a clearer vision of looking back than forward and it is often much more pleasant." Fortunately, Gladys acted on her impulse to "look back." Perhaps she recognized, as an amateur historian, that her own experiences and those of her family reflected the tremendous challenges and changes that had taken place in the twentieth century. She and Ray and their children had shared the satisfaction and heartaches of farm life through depression and prosperity. They had survived two world wars and, like other Americans, had witnessed the growth of American power and of Americans' worldliness. They had rejoiced in the early days over technologies now deemed primitive—Gladys's beautiful new wood-burning stove in 1921, for instance—but eventually grew accustomed to color televisions and jet planes. Whereas Ray and Gladys had struggled to visit what to them were exotic places like the Rocky Mountains or Yellowstone National Park or Los Angeles, their progeny traveled throughout the United States and all over the world.

If all of this sounds familiar, it is simply because Gladys's stories—and the rainbows she and her family chased—comprise a microcosm of the American experience in this century, especially for the Northern Plains. They go beyond one family's nostalgia to provide the kind of grass roots history that lurks beneath the surface of the major events and abstract trends that dominate the historical consciousness of most Americans. Her stories are, in short, the stories of millions of other men and women who, rather than "making" history, merely lived it.

Bibliography

NEWSPAPERS

Aberdeen (South Dakota) *Evening News*
Dakota Farmer (Aberdeen, South Dakota)
Inwood (Iowa) *Herald*
Lyman County (South Dakota) *Herald*
Madison (South Dakota) *Daily Leader*
Sioux Falls (South Dakota) *Argus Leader*

PUBLISHED SOURCES

Allen, Frederick Lewis. *Since Yesterday: The 1930s in America.* New York: Harper and Row/Perennial Library, 1940.
Anderson, Oscar Edward. *Refrigeration in America: A History of a New Technology and Its Impact.* Princeton: Princeton Univ. Press, 1953.
Annual Report of the South Dakota Department of Agriculture, 1958. Pierre: State of South Dakota, 1958.
Armitage, Susan, and Elizabeth Jameson, eds. *The Women's West.* Norman: Univ. of Oklahoma Press, 1987.
Belasco, Warren James. *Americans on the Road: From Autocamp to Motel, 1910–1945.* Cambridge, Mass.: MIT Press, 1979.
Bogart, Leo. *The Age of Television: A Study of Viewing Habits and the Impact of Television on American Life.* New York: Frederick Ungar, 1956.
Brown, D. Clayton. *Electricity for Rural America: The Fight for the REA.* Westport, Conn.: Greenwood Press, 1980.
Bureau of the Census. *Abstract of the Fourteenth Census of the United States, 1920.* Washington, D.C.: U.S. Government Printing Office, 1923.
———. *Fifteenth Census of the United States, 1930: Vol. 1. Population.* Washington, D.C.: U.S. Government Printing Office, 1931.

————. *Census of Agriculture, 1940 – South Dakota.* Washington, D.C.: U.S. Government Printing Office, 1942.

————. *Statistical Abstract of the United States, 1950.* Washington, D.C.: U.S. Government Printing Office, 1954.

————. *Statistical Abstract of the United States, 1964.* Washington, D.C.: U.S. Government Printing Office, 1964.

Cowan, Ruth Schwartz. *More Work for Mother: The Ironies of Household Technology from Open Hearth to the Microwave.* New York: Basic Books, 1983.

Cox, T. Hillard, and L. M. Brown. "South Dakota Farm Prices, 1890–1937." Bulletin 317. Brookings: Agricultural Experiment Station and South Dakota State College, 1938.

Cummins, Cedric. *The University of South Dakota, 1862–1966.* Vermillion: Dakota Press, 1975.

Current, Richard N. *The History of Wisconsin: The Civil War Era, 1848–1873.* Madison: State Historical Society of Wisconsin, 1976.

Dodd, Donald B., and Wynelle S. Dodd. *Historical Statistics of the United States, 1790–1970: Vol. 2. The Midwest.* University, Ala.: Univ. of Alabama Press, 1976.

Dorsey, Jean Muir, and Maxwell Jay Dorsey, comps. *Christopher Gist of Maryland and Some of His Descendants, 1679–1957.* Chicago: John S. Swift, 1969.

Edwards, Everett. "The Need for Historical Materials for Agricultural Research." *Agricultural History* 9 (January 1935): 3–11.

Federal Writers' Project of the Work Projects Administration, State of South Dakota. *A South Dakota Guide.* Pierre: State Publishing Co., 1938.

Fink, Deborah. *Open Country, Iowa: Rural Women, Tradition and Change.* Albany: State Univ. of New York Press, 1986.

Fischer, Christine, ed. *Let Them Speak for Themselves: Women in the American West, 1849–1900.* Hamden, Conn.: Shoe String Press, 1977.

Fite, Gilbert C. "Great Plains Farming: A Century of Change and Development." *Agricultural History* 51(January 1977): 244–56.

————. *American Farmers: The New Minority.* Bloomington: Indiana Univ. Press, 1981.

————. "The Transformation of South Dakota Agriculture: The Effects of Mechanization, 1939–1964." *South Dakota History* 19 (Fall 1989): 278–305.

Fricken, Robert E., and Charles P. LeWarne. *Washington: A Centennial History.* Seattle: Univ. of Washington Press, 1988.

Friedberger, Mark. *Farm Families and Change in Twentieth-Century America.* Lexington: Univ. Press of Kentucky, 1988.

Grant, H. Roger, and L. Edward Purcell, eds. *Years of Struggle: The Farm Diary of Elmer G. Powers, 1931–1936.* Ames: Iowa State Univ. Press, 1976.

Hamilton, Carl. *In No Time at All.* Ames: Iowa State Univ. Press, 1974.

Hampsten, Elizabeth. *Read This Only to Yourself: The Private Writings of Midwestern Women, 1880–1910.* Bloomington: Indiana Univ. Press, 1982.

Howard, Robert P. *Illinois: A History of the Prairie State.* Grand Rapids, Mich.: William B. Erdmans, 1972.

Illinois Federal Writers' Project, Work Projects Administration. *Illinois: A Descriptive and Historical Guide,* rev. ed. Chicago: A. C. McClung, 1947.

Inwood Centennial Book Committee. *Inwood's First 100 Years, 1884–1984.* Dallas: National ShareGraphics, 1984.

Jahr, Dale. *Lake County Pictorial History.* Madison, S.Dak.: Prairie Historical Society, 1976.

Jellison, Katherine. "Women and Technology on the Great Plains, 1900–1940." *Great Plains Quarterly* 8 (Summer 1988): 145–57.

Jennings, Dana Close. *Free Ice Water! The Story of Wall Drug.* Aberdeen, S.Dak.: North Plains Press, 1969.

Karolevitz, Robert F. *The Prairie is My Garden: The Story of Harvey Dunn, Artist.* Aberdeen, S.Dak.: North Plains Press, 1969.

Kumlien, W. F. "A Graphic Summary of the Relief Situation in South Dakota (1930–1935)." Bulletin 310. Brookings: Agricultural Experiment Station, South Dakota State College, 1934.

————. "The Rural Health Situation in South Dakota." Bulletin 258. Brookings: Agricultural Experiment Station, South Dakota State College, 1937.

Lambert, Roger. "New Deal Experiences in Production Control: The Livestock Program, 1933–1935." Ph.D. diss., Univ. of Oklahoma, 1962.

Landis, Paul H. *Rural Relief in South Dakota.* Brookings: Agricultural Experiment Station, South Dakota State College, 1934.

LeCompte, Janet. *Emily: The Diary of a Hard-Worked Woman.* Lincoln: Univ. of Nebraska Press, 1987.

Leiffer, Murray and Dorothy. *Enter the Old Portals: Reminiscences — Fifty Years on a Seminary Campus.* Evanston, Ill.: Bureau of Social and Religious Research, 1987.

Low, Ann Marie. *Dust Bowl Diary.* Lincoln: Univ. of Nebraska Press, 1984.

Lowry, V. A. *Forty Years at General Beadle, 1922–1962.* Madison: Dakota State College, 1984.

Lundy, Gabriel. "Farm Mortgage Experience in South Dakota, 1910–
    1940." Bulletin 370. Brookings: Agricultural Experiment Station,
    South Dakota State College, 1943.
Malone, Michael P., ed. *Historians and the American West.* Lincoln:
    Univ. of Nebraska Press, 1983.
Millett, Allan R., and Peter Maslowski. *For the Common Defense: A
    Military History of the United States of America.* New York: Free
    Press, 1984.
Morris, John W. *Ghost Towns of Oklahoma.* Norman: Univ. of Okla-
    homa Press, 1977.
Munn, Glenn G. *Encyclopedia of Banking & Commerce,* 8th ed. Bos-
    ton: Bankers Publishing Co., 1983.
Myers, Sandra L. *Westering Women and the Frontier Experience,
    1800–1915.* Albuquerque: Univ. of New Mexico Press, 1982.
Nelson, Paula M. *After the West Was Won: Homesteaders and Town-
    Builders in Western South Dakota, 1900–1917.* Iowa City: Univ.
    of Iowa Press, 1986.
Niswander, Kenneth R. *Obstetrics: Essentials of Clinical Practice.* Bos-
    ton: Little, Brown, 1976.
Norwood, Frederick A. *From Dawn to Midday at Garrett.* Evanston,
    Ill.: Garrett Evangelical Theological Seminary, 1978.
Oshkosh: One Hundred Years a City, 1853–1953. Oshkosh, Wisc.: Cas-
    tle-Pierce Printing Co., 1953.
Pressley, Thomas J., and William H. Scofield. *Farm Real Estate Values
    in the United States by Counties, 1850–1959.* Seattle: Univ. of
    Washington Press, 1965.
Putz, Paul, ed. *Historic Sites of South Dakota: A Guidebook.* Vermil-
    lion: Business Research Bureau, University of South Dakota, and
    Historical Preservation Center, 1980.
Riley, Glenda. *The Female Frontier: A Comparative View of Women
    on the Prairie and the Plains.* Lawrence: Univ. Press of Kansas,
    1988.
Schell, Herbert. *History of South Dakota,* 3d ed. Lincoln: Univ. of
    Nebraska Press, 1975.
Schlesinger, Arthur S., Jr. *The Politics of Upheaval.* Boston: Houghton
    Mifflin, 1960.
Schlissel, Lillian, ed. *Women's Diaries of the Westward Journey.* New
    York: Schocken Books, 1982.
Schwieder, Dorothy. "Education and Change in the Lives of Iowa Farm
    Women, 1900–1940." *Agricultural History* 60 (Spring 1986): 200–
    15.
Schwieder, Dorothy, and Deborah Fink. "Plains Women: Rural Life in
    the 1930s." *Great Plains Quarterly* 8 (Spring 1988): 79–88.
Severson, Harlan M. *Stepping Forward, Boldly: The Story of East*

River Electric Power Cooperative. Madison, S. Dak.: Hunter Publishing, 1975.

South Dakota: Fifty Years of Progress, 1889–1939. Sioux Falls: South Dakota Golden Anniversary Book Co., 1939.

The Spectator [Inwood High School yearbook]. Inwood: Inwood Herald Print, 1915 and 1916.

Springer, Marlene, and Haskell Springer, eds. *Plains Woman: The Diary of Martha Farnsworth, 1882–1922.* Bloomington: Indiana Univ. Press, 1986.

Stratton, Joanna L. *Pioneer Women: Voices from the Kansas Frontier.* New York: Simon and Schuster, 1981.

Time Magazine. *Time Capsule: 1944.* New York: Time-Life Books, 1967.

Tweton, D. Jerome. *The New Deal at the Grass Roots: Programs For the People in Otter Tail County, Minnesota.* St. Paul: Minnesota Historical Society Press, 1988.

U.S. Department of Agriculture. *Yearbook of Agriculture, 1921.* Washington, D.C.: U.S. Government Printing Office, 1922.

———. *Yearbook of Agriculture, 1933.* Washington, D.C.: U.S. Government Printing Office, 1933.

———. *Science in Farming: Yearbook of Agriculture, 1943–1947.* Washington, D.C.: U.S. Government Printing Office, 1947.

———. *Animal Disease: Yearbook of Agriculture, 1956.* Washington, D.C.: U.S. Government Printing Office, 1956.

———. *After a Hundred Years: Yearbook of Agriculture, 1962.* Washington, D.C.: U.S. Government Printing Office, 1962.

Utah Writers' Project, Work Projects Administration. *Utah: A Guide to the State.* New York: Hastings House, 1941.

Vogel, John. "Great Lakes Lumber on the Great Plains: Laird, Norton Lumber Company in South Dakota." Ph.D. diss., Marquette Univ., 1989.

Weigley, Russell F. *History of the United States Army.* Bloomington: Indiana Univ. Press, 1984.

Wertz, Dorothy. *Lying-In: A History of Childbirth in America.* New York: Free Press, 1977.

Wik, Reynold M. "The Radio in Rural America During the 1920s." *Agricultural History* 55 (October 1981): 339–50.

Winkler, Allan M. *Home Front, U.S. A.: Americans during World War II.* Arlington Heights, Ill.: Harlan Davidson, 1986.

Winters, Donald L. *Farmers Without Farms: Agricultural Tenancy in Nineteenth Century Iowa.* Westport, Conn.: Greenwood Press, 1978.

World War II History Commission. *South Dakota in World War II.* Pierre, S.Dak.: World War II History Commission, ca. 1947.

Leffler Family

McCracken Family

George Watson Leffler —— Elizabeth Van Horne

Jerome B. McCracken —— Minerva Ann Sa
(1874–1908)   (1849–1931)

Mary Joanna, Eva, George Theodore,
Willis, Lucy Adeline, LeRoy, Frank Watson Leffler
(1869–1934)

Rhodemia McCracken, Louisa, Evalina, Ola, Fre
(1871–1951)   Leonard, Lee, Cor

Sylvia Ethel
(1892–1983)

Gladys Urbana Leffler
(1898–1989)

Lee Theodore
(1904–1968)

Ira Leonard
(1909–1959)

Kent (1922–   ) m. Edith Ingalls
    Sara (1949–   )
    Melissa (1952–   )
    John (1956–   )

Rodney Raymond (1926–   ) m. Doris Leivestad
    Barbara (1954–   )
    Linda (1956–   )

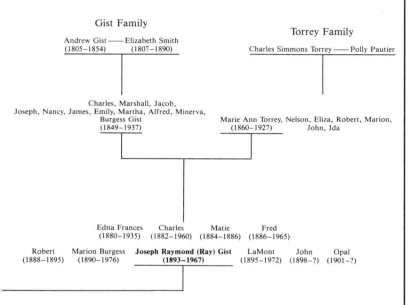

Gist Family

Andrew Gist ——— Elizabeth Smith
(1805–1854)   (1807–1890)

Torrey Family

Charles Simmons Torrey ——— Polly Pautier

Charles, Marshall, Jacob,
Joseph, Nancy, James, Emily, Martha, Alfred, Minerva,
Burgess Gist
(1849–1937)

Marie Ann Torrey, Nelson, Eliza, Robert, Marion,
(1860–1927)   John, Ida

Edna Frances   Charles   Matie   Fred
(1880–1935) (1882–1960) (1884–1886) (1886–1965)

Robert   Marion Burgess   **Joseph Raymond (Ray) Gist**   LaMont   John   Opal
(1888–1895) (1890–1976)   **(1893–1967)**   (1895–1972) (1898–?) (1901–?)

Ruth (1931–) m. Robert Spencer
   Kirby (1959–)
   Lee (1962–)

FAMILY TREE.